MW00770457

—HOW TO USE A—
CRYSTAL

About the Author

Richard Webster was born and raised in New Zealand. He has been interested in the psychic world since he was nine years old. As a teenager, he became involved in hypnotism and later became a professional stage hypnotist. After school, he worked in the publishing business and purchased a bookstore. The concept of reincarnation played a significant role in his decision to become a past-life specialist. Richard has also taught psychic development classes, which are based on many of his books.

Richard's first book was published in 1972, fulfilling a childhood dream of becoming an author. Richard is now the author of over a hundred books, and is still writing today. His bestselling books include *Spirit Guides & Angel Guardians* and *Creative Visualization for Beginners*.

Richard has appeared on several radio and TV programs in the United States and abroad. He currently resides in New Zealand with his wife and three children. He regularly travels the world to give lectures, hold workshops, and continue his research.

HOW TO USE A
CRYSTAL

50 Practical Rituals and Spiritual Activities
for Inspiration and Wellbeing

RICHARD
WEBSTER

Llewellyn Worldwide
Woodbury, Minnesota

FIRST EDITION
First Printing, 2018

Book design by Bob Gaul
Cover design by Kristi Carlson
Editing by Annie Burdick

Llewellyn Publications is a registered trademark of Llewellyn Worldwide Ltd.

Library of Congress Cataloging-in-Publication Data (Pending)
ISBN: 978-0-7387-5670-7

Llewellyn Worldwide Ltd. does not participate in, endorse, or have any authority or responsibility concerning private business transactions between our authors and the public.
  All mail addressed to the author is forwarded, but the publisher cannot, unless specifically instructed by the author, give out an address or phone number.
  Any internet references contained in this work are current at publication time, but the publisher cannot guarantee that a specific location will continue to be maintained. Please refer to the publisher's website for links to authors' websites and other sources.

Llewellyn Publications
A Division of Llewellyn Worldwide Ltd.
2143 Wooddale Drive
Woodbury, MN 55125-2989
www.llewellyn.com

Printed in the United States of America

CONTENTS

For my good friend
Lary Kuehn
Who knows more about
crystals than anyone else I've ever met.

INTRODUCTION

Every now and again, people ask me what they can do with a crystal. Usually the question comes from someone who's been given a crystal or happened to buy one, but occasionally I get asked this question by people who've been involved with crystals for many years.

I used to suggest that they spend time with their crystal, get to know it, and then ask it how it wants to be used. I could see in their faces that this wasn't particularly helpful, and I was forced to come up with a better reply.

Now when people ask me what they can do with their crystal, I ask them what *they* would like to do with it. Some people have a clear answer, and I can help them get started with whatever it happens to be. Most people aren't sure, and I recite a list of possibilities: "Health, love, money, creativity, spiritual growth, forgiveness, luck, and your home."

Usually that's enough to get people started, and I feel just as excited as they are when they decide what they're going to do.

This book developed from that list of possibilities. There are fifty suggestions here, and I hope you'll find some that appeal to you.

All you need is one crystal.

PART 1

◆

SOME CRYSTAL
BASICS

1

◆

CRYSTALS AND GEMSTONES

There is so much to learn about the stones we admire and love. Here we will take a look at the differences between crystals and gemstones, as well as their historical and modern uses. I will also share a bit about how I was first introduced to their gifts and how we can make use of the wonderful energy they have to share.

Historical Use

Throughout history, people have been fascinated with crystals and gemstones. Because of their beauty, they were probably originally worn for decorative purposes, but it wouldn't have taken long for people to discover their spiritual aspects, as crystals can provide serenity and peace of mind. Using crystals for divination and healing would have been a logical extension of this.

Because crystals have always been valuable, people of influence wore them as symbols of power and authority. It's recorded in the book of Exodus that Aaron, the High Priest of Israel, wore a twelve-jeweled breastplate. One of the jewels was an amethyst. Today, bishops in the Catholic Church usually have an amethyst in their episcopal rings. A king's crown is bedecked with precious gemstones to help him rule wisely and to demonstrate his supremacy. Stones and crystals were also valued by the ancient Sumerians, Mesopotamians, and Egyptians. A 7,500-year-old gold and turquoise bracelet was found adorning the mummy of an ancient Egyptian queen (Knuth 1999, 1).

The first serious study of crystals appeared in about 300 BCE. This was called *On Stones*, and was written by Theophrastus, a student of Aristotle. Scientific study of crystals began in 1546, when Georgius Agricola published his *De Natura Fossilium*. Ten years later, *De Re Metallica* was posthumously published, and it was used by the mining industry for more than two hundred years. In 1837, James Dwight Dana (1813-1895), an American scientist, suggested a system of mineral classification based on structure and chemical makeup in his book *System of Mineralogy*.

Crystals have always been valued in North and South America for spiritual and healing qualities. The Mayans used obsidian to make ceremonial knives and ancient Mexicans formed mirrors from pyrite.

Crystals have also been revered in India for thousands of years. The system of placing crystals on chakras began here, and they also used them to help remedy negative aspects in people's horoscopes.

Numerous legends have been created about crystals. One I particularly like was the belief of early Christians that crystal quartz was originally holy water from heaven that was transformed into ice as it traveled to earth. Angels petrified the ice to prevent it from melting, so it could be used to protect and look after all of humanity. Interestingly, the word crystal comes from *krystallos*, a Greek word meaning ice. Thousands of years ago, people thought that crystals were made of ice that had frozen so hard that it would never melt. The Roman scholar Pliny the Elder (23-79 CE) wrote that "a violently contracting coldness forms the rock crystal in the same way as ice" (Glazer 2016, ii). The ancient Greeks believed that all quartz crystals were fragments of the crystal of truth that Hercules dropped to earth from Mount Olympus.

One charming legend says that if you dig into the ground at the end of a rainbow you'll find a piece of turquoise. Interestingly, Native Americans and Tibetans shared a belief that turquoise joined heaven and earth.

Modern Use

Crystals were, and still are, used as amulets and lucky charms. I wear an amulet of green jade around my neck for a variety of reasons, including protection and luck. It also reminds me every day of the friend who made it for me.

Crystals play an essential role in modern-day technology. Many things we take for granted, such as computers, cell phones, quartz watches, credit cards, laser technology, fiber-optic phone lines, solar energy, and televisions, all need crystals to make them work.

Personal Introduction to Crystals

Most people become interested in crystals by chance. Maybe they were given one or happened to see an attractive crystal and bought it because of its beauty. I was given my first quartz crystal when I was about twenty. It wasn't beautiful to look at, but I felt relaxed and peaceful whenever I held it. I knew nothing about crystals at the time and asked other people to hold it, to see if they experienced the same sensations that I did. Some did and some didn't.

About a year after that, I was at an airport waiting for a flight and got into conversation with a man a few years older than me. When we lined up to board the plane, he gave me a tiny crystal with a broken point. He told me it was a warrior crystal that would help me tame the warrior within and enable me to lead a good, productive life. I was embarrassed to receive this gift from a stranger, but his gift and what he told me about the crystal provided the necessary impetus for me to start studying crystals.

Since then I've owned hundreds of crystals. Some remain in my possession for a year or two, others I keep for decades. Sooner or later, though, I pass my crystals on to people who I think will benefit from them. However, I do still have the two unglamorous pieces of quartz crystal that started me off on this quest.

The Energy of Crystals

No matter what they look like, all quartz crystals vibrate to a phenomenon called the piezoelectric effect, which was discovered by Pierre Curie (1859-1906), a Nobel Prize–winning French physicist, and his brother Jacques. Pierre was also married to Marie Curie, the discoverer of radium. The Curie brothers found that when a crystal is placed under stress, an electric charge is produced across its surface. You can do this with your own crystal. If you hold it tightly, you'll place it under stress and cause the electromagnetic force to act (Katzir 2006, 15-16).

The Differences between Gemstones and Crystals

People sometimes get confused about gemstones and crystals. Gemstones are beautiful and durable, and are usually used for ornamental and decorative purposes. They're cut, faceted, polished, and placed into an item of jewelry. Conversely, a crystal is a solid substance whose molecules are arranged in a geometric pattern, with a symmetrical arrangement of faces. Every face of a crystal has its double lying parallel to it on the other side. Sugar and salt are both examples of crystals, but they're not gemstones. Quartz is by far the most common crystal and can be found all over the world. Gemstones are usually more valuable than crystals. Most gemstones are also crystals, but there are exceptions. Amber, coral, pearl, and turquoise are gemstones, but they're organic in origin and aren't crystals.

The aim of this book is to give you a variety of uses for a crystal. It doesn't matter what type of crystal it happens to be.

2

◆

CHOOSING YOUR CRYSTAL

If you don't already own any crystals, the chances are high that you'll gradually build up a collection once you start actively working with them. However, for the purposes of this book, you need only one crystal. It doesn't matter what crystal you choose, as long as you feel it will work well with you and for you. That's why it's important to choose it carefully.

There are many places where you can buy crystals, such as new age stores, rock and mineral stores, lapidary (gemstone) suppliers, rock and gem shows, craft fairs, flea markets, and natural history museums. You can also buy them online, though I have never done this, as I like to examine and hold the crystal before buying it.

You may find it helpful to take a book with you when you're searching for crystals, as not every lapidary store has staff who are interested in the spiritual or healing qualities of crystals.

It's considered good etiquette to ask before handling other people's crystals, even in a store. Many people dislike others handling their crystals, and you need to respect this.

There are many ways to choose a crystal, but I believe that it is the crystal that chooses you. On many occasions I've set out to buy a certain crystal but arrived home with something completely different, as I became attracted to a different stone. Whenever I forced myself to stick to my original plan and buy a particular stone, I was never happy with my purchase, and have sometimes returned to the store later to buy the stone that "called out" to me.

Choosing a crystal is much like making a friend. You probably get on with many people but have a much smaller number that you call friends. It's more fun to work on a project with people you like than it is to work with strangers or casual acquaintances. When you find the right crystal, it will become your friend.

It's best not to have any preconceived ideas when you start looking for a crystal. Visit a store that sells crystals and see if one of them feels right for you. Many people choose a quartz crystal for their first stone, but you can choose any stone that appeals to you. Take your time when shopping for a crystal. You don't have to buy one from the first place you visit, and you should not buy any stone that you have the slightest doubt about.

When you find a stone that appeals to you, feel its energy. You can do this by placing it in the palm of your left hand and covering it gently with your right palm. Focus your attention on the palms of your hands and see what thoughts, feelings, and sensations come to you. It's a good sign if the crystal feels as if it already belongs to you. Follow your intuition. If a crystal feels right for you, it will be. Do this process with several stones before buying one.

There are other ways to hold a crystal when you're testing it. You might choose to place the crystal in the palm of one hand and gently close the fingers of that hand over it. You might prefer to hold it between your thumb and index finger. You might even like to place it on a flat surface, with your palms facing each other, one or two inches away from the stone.

A good friend of mine chooses his crystals by standing in front of a selection of stones. He closes his eyes for a few moments and relaxes his body. When he opens his eyes, he chooses the first crystal his eyes are drawn to.

Not every crystal shop will allow you to handle their stones. When this occurs, pass your right hand over any crystals that interest you and see which ones respond to your energy. Usually you'll experience a feeling of warmth when your hand is over a crystal that harmonizes with you. This means you'd work well with it.

If you like two stones and can't decide which one to buy, place one of them slightly to your left and the other slightly to your right. Close your eyes, take a few slow, deep breaths, and ask yourself, "Which of these stones would be better for me right now?" You'll probably feel your entire body leaning slightly in the direction of the stone that would be better for you. If you don't feel anything, wait a few seconds and open your eyes. Don't move. Notice the way you're standing and sense if your body is indicating either of the stones. This process is called body dowsing, since instead of a pendulum or divining rod, you're using your entire body to indicate the stone that would be better for you.

You can use body dowsing whenever you want to make a choice between two or more objects. When I'm looking for a book on a certain subject in a bookstore, for instance, and can't decide which one to buy, I'll use body dowsing to help make the right decision.

The crystal you buy doesn't have to be perfect. Large, perfect stones may look magnificent, but they're usually expensive. If you have a limited budget you might need to choose a stone that contains flaws or imperfections. These won't affect anything you choose to do with the stone. In fact, you're likely to fall in love with its flaws, as they add to the charm and personality of the stone. In addition, you may find that the flawed crystal provides better energy than the apparently perfect one.

Once you've chosen a stone, you'll have to get to know it. Carrying it around with you enables you to gain rapport with it. Talk to your crystal and listen carefully for any replies. You'll be surprised at what thoughts come into your mind when you work with crystals.

As you become familiar with your stone, you'll be able to use it to gain energy or confidence whenever you need it. All you need to do is stroke it and silently ask for whatever it is you want. You'll be able to use your crystal whenever you are bothered by a problem or concern. Your stone will help you remain peaceful and calm, and enable you to solve whatever it happens to be without becoming agitated or stressed.

Once you find the right crystal for you, it will protect and guide you in everything you do.

3

◆

LOOKING AFTER YOUR CRYSTAL

Crystals need to be treated with love and respect. One of the best ways to do this is to cleanse your crystal on a regular basis. This removes any negative energies that could be affecting it. It is especially important to cleanse your crystal when you first obtain it, as this gets rid of any energies it may have picked up before coming into your possession.

Cleansing Your Crystal

Some people refuse to let other people handle their crystals because they feel the crystals could pick up negative energy through these contacts. If this is the case, there's also a good chance that the crystals will be picking up good energies as well. Consequently, I don't mind if other people handle my crystals. In fact, when doing crystal readings with a number of crystals, I encourage people to touch and handle the ones they are drawn to. People are attracted to them and want to feel and hold them. I'm happy for them to do this, as it's a simple matter to cleanse them afterward.

Crystals and gemstones need to be cleansed regularly, as they absorb all the energies, good and bad, that surround them. Stones are like batteries that absorb energy and pass it on. Cleansing eliminates all the negativity and bad vibrations that the crystal has absorbed from its environment and the people who have interacted with it. This is why crystals that are used for healing purposes need to be cleansed before and after they're used, as any negative energy remaining in the crystal will affect its ability to heal.

When Should a Stone Be Cleansed?

You should cleanse your stone as soon as possible after you've bought it. This is to eliminate any negativity it may have picked up before you purchased it. You should cleanse it before and after using it. You should also cleanse it whenever you feel it has become dull and needs a boost of positivity.

Gemstones that are worn should be cleansed every day. Stones that are used for healing should be cleansed after they have been used. Stones that are used as pendulums should be cleansed after every use, too. Stones that are used to cleanse the environment, decorative stones, and protective stones should be cleansed at least once a month. Stones should also be cleansed whenever they feel dull or appear to have lost energy and power.

Cleaning Crystals and Gemstones

Your intention is the most important part of a cleansing. Consequently, no matter which method you use, you should hold the intention in your mind that the process will remove all the negativity that surrounds the stone.

There are many ways to cleanse stones. Here is a baker's dozen of the most popular methods. Use your intuition to decide which method to use. You may decide on one method and use it every time you cleanse a crystal. Alternatively, you might use a different method each time.

Another possibility is to combine two or three different methods. These methods all work well with each other and ensure that your crystal is totally free of any negativity.

Water

Water is a popular method for cleansing stones but needs to be used carefully. Leaving your crystal out in the rain is a good way to cleanse it using water. The easiest way to cleanse your crystal is to hold it, point downward, under room temperature running water for three or four minutes while thinking of your desire or intent for the crystal to be completely cleansed of all negative energy. Gently dry the crystal with a cotton or linen cloth and place it in the open air for an hour or two.

This method works well for most purposes, but there are times when you'll want to give your crystal a stronger cleansing. You should do this whenever you obtain a new crystal, whenever the crystal is exposed to negative emotions, whenever the crystal has been used for healing purposes, for any crystal you wear or carry with you daily, and whenever you have an intuition that your crystal needs to be cleansed.

You should also cleanse your crystal if you've been using it for one purpose and are intending to use it for a different purpose. You should, for instance, cleanse your crystal if you've been working on one chapter of this book and decide to start experimenting with the material in another chapter. This process is called *dedication*, as the stone is being dedicated to a specific purpose.

Use room temperature water. Warm, hot, or cold water may damage your crystal. Make sure that your crystal will not be affected by water, as soft stones can be damaged by water. These include angelite, azulite, howlite, malachite, and selenite.

Smudging

This is my favorite method. All you need is a smudge stick made of sage, cedar, or sweetgrass. Sage is my favorite. Smudge sticks can be obtained from wellness and new age stores and online. Smudge sticks are easy to make, and it's satisfying to make them from herbs that you have grown and dried yourself. Instructions are available online. You need to be careful when using smudge sticks, as they give off a great deal of heat. Once the smudge stick is burning, pass your crystal through the smoke several times.

If you don't have a smudge stick, you can pass your crystal through the smoke produced by a candle.

Sage Bath

You can also use dried sage to cleanse your crystal. Fill a drinking glass with dried sage and bury your crystal in it for twenty-four hours. Sage is extremely good at neutralizing negative energy and replacing it with positivity. Use the sage only once. After it's been used, dispose of the sage by burning or burying it.

If you wish, you can use dried rose petals, frankincense, myrrh, sandalwood, or any combination of dried herbs instead of sage.

Sun and the Moon

Exposing your gemstone to the rays of the sun or the moon is a powerful way to cleanse your stone. Place your crystal where it will receive the full rays of the sun for about an hour, or expose it to the rays of the moon for at least one night. Whenever possible, I like to expose the crystal to both the sun's and moon's rays for twenty-four hours.

You should cleanse amethyst, celestite, opal, and turquoise in the rays of the moon, as the rays of the sun can cause the colors to fade.

Earth
Burying your crystal, point downward, in the earth for one or two days is a good way to cleanse it. You can bury it outside in your garden or indoors using the earth surrounding a potted plant. If you bury it outdoors, make sure to mark the spot so you can find it again without any difficulty.

Salt
Burying your crystal in a glass container of raw salt for at least twenty-four hours is a popular way to cleanse crystals. Household salt works well, but many people prefer to use rock or sea salt. Be careful when cleansing with salt, as it can damage the surface and texture of some stones.

Sound
Pleasing sounds are a useful way to cleanse crystals. The pure note of a Tibetan singing bowl, the gentle sound of meditation music, the vibrant sound of a gong, or the devotion of someone chanting are all good ways to cleanse crystals.

Prayer
A simple prayer to the Universal Life Force is a highly effective way to clear your crystal. Hold the crystal in your

cupped hands and say a prayer along the lines of, "Infinite Spirit (God, Goddess, or your own name for the Divine), please clear all the negative energies inside this crystal, so that it can be used for the good of everyone. Thank you. Amen." If you prefer, you could recite a mantra or a traditional prayer, such as the Lord's Prayer.

Breath

You can cleanse your crystal by blowing on it with the intent of cleansing it. Hold the crystal in your cupped hands and exhale onto it. Turn the crystal around to make sure that every part of it receives some of your breath. It doesn't matter how long you do this for. The only essential is that you remain focused on your intent while doing it. This is a useful method to remember if you need to cleanse your crystal quickly.

Not long ago, a friend showed me how she cleanses her crystal using breath. She holds the crystal to her heart while inhaling. She then brings the crystal to her mouth and blows on it while exhaling. She does this seven times, turning the crystal each time to make sure that every part of it receives her breath.

Brown Rice

Burying your crystal overnight in a bowl of brown rice is a simple yet effective way to cleanse it. In the morning, gently wipe your crystal with a soft cloth, and dispose of the brown rice. Do not eat it, as it will have absorbed the negativity it has removed from your stone. I prefer brown rice, but white rice is also effective.

Crystal Cluster

If you're fortunate enough to have access to a crystal cluster of amethyst or quartz, you can place your crystal on or inside it overnight.

Freezing

A little-known method to cleanse your crystal is to place it inside a freezer for three to four hours.

Visualization

Place your crystal in your right hand. Hold your left hand, palm up, as high as you can. Visualize divine energy entering your body through your left palm, and then sense it radiating out of your right palm to purify and cleanse your crystal.

Energizing Your Crystal

In addition to cleansing your crystal you should also energize it by placing it in direct sunlight for five to six hours a week. If you have more than one crystal you can energize them by keeping them close together.

Dedicating Your Crystal

You need to dedicate your crystal whenever you decide to use it for a particular task. If, for instance, you've been using your crystal to attract love and have now decided to use it to enhance your memory, you'll need to dedicate it to its new task.

Start by thinking of a short phrase or sentence that encapsulates what you want your crystal to do. As this phrase is effectively an intention, I usually start the phrase with the words "I intend this crystal," followed by exactly what I desire.

In the case of memory, I might want to become better at remembering names, or maybe remembering vocabulary in a foreign language. In this case, I'd say something along the lines of "I intend this crystal to improve my ability to remember people's names," or "I intend this crystal to enable me to effortlessly memorize and retain German vocabulary." If I want to improve my overall memory I might say "I intend this crystal to enable me to improve my memory in every area of my life."

Once you have your intention clear in your mind, sit down and relax, with your crystal in your hands. I like to sit with the crystal resting between the palms of my hands, which I hold at waist level in a praying position. Repeat your phrase several times, either silently or out loud. I prefer to do it out loud, as I find it helpful to hear the words as well as say them. However, you might prefer to say them silently if other people are nearby.

Repeat this dedication every day for about a week to ensure that the crystal is properly programmed. You can use your crystal as soon as you've dedicated it once, but you'll achieve better results if you use repetition. A few minutes every day for a week is sufficient.

The most important part of the dedication is the intention. Theoretically you can perform the dedication without the crystal being present, as long as you're able to visualize it clearly. In practice, though, everyone I know who works with crystals always has some form of physical contact with their crystal while dedicating it.

One person I know holds her crystal against the third eye in her forehead. Another holds it against her heart. I'm friends with a crystal healer who places the crystal horizontally on a tabletop and rests both forefingers on it while stating his intention. Many people hold the base of the crystal in their left hand and cup their right palm over the tip of the crystal. Some people hold their cupped right hand an inch or so above the crystal, while others prefer the palm of the right hand to be in contact with it.

Even if you have no immediate purpose for your crystal, you should still dedicate it. You can do this by holding it in the palms of your hands while sending thoughts of love and peace to it. Tell it that it is dedicated to all tasks that involve kindness and love to all, and that it will be a source of positive energy whenever you need it. If possible, repeat this seven times a day, for seven days.

Keeping Your Crystal

As much as possible, keep your crystal where it will receive sunlight and fresh air. Crystals like natural surfaces, like wood, glass, silk, and other natural fibers. You can transport your crystals in closed boxes, but they should not be kept in jewelry boxes, drawers, or any other closed environment.

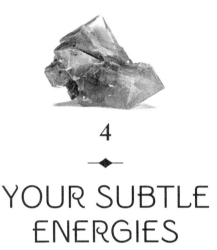

4

◆

YOUR SUBTLE
ENERGIES

Surrounding the human body is an energy field called the aura. Although it surrounds the body, it's also part of every cell in the body and reflects all the subtle life energies. Consequently, it should be considered an extension of the body, rather than just something that surrounds it. The energies that flow through our aura reflect our personality, thoughts, and emotions. They also reveal our mental, physical, and spiritual well-being.

Inside the aura are swirling circles of energy known as chakras. *Chakra* is a Sanskrit word that means *wheel*. The chakras can be thought of as batteries that connect our physical and subtle bodies. They absorb the higher energies and transform them into a form that can be utilized in the physical body. There are seven major chakras spaced along the length of the spinal column. Each is concerned with different functions of the body, and the organs associated with them.

The Chakras

Root Chakra
Color: Red
Element: Earth
Sense: Smell
Desires: Physical contact
Challenge: To think before acting
Keyword: Physical

The root chakra is situated at the base of the spine and provides feelings of security and comfort. The root chakra keeps us firmly grounded to the earth. It makes us feel joyful, vibrant, alive, and full of energy. At an emotional level, the root chakra provides courage and persistence. It also governs our sense of smell and the solid parts of the body, such as the teeth, nails, and bones. It plays an important role in our survival, as it also governs our fight-or-flight responses.

When this chakra is understimulated we feel nervous and insecure. As a result, fear can gather inside this chakra.

When it's overstimulated, we can be overbearing, selfish, domineering, and addicted to money or sex.

Useful stones for the root chakra include fire agate, bloodstone, red calcite, garnet, heliotrope, hematite, red jasper, red quartz, ruby, and smoky topaz

Sacral Chakra
Color: Orange
Element: Water
Sense: Taste
Desires: Respect and acceptance
Challenge: To love and serve others
Keyword: Social

The sacral chakra is situated at the level of the sacrum in the small of the back, about two inches below the navel. Because it relates to the element of water, the sacral chakra is concerned with the fluidic functions of the body. It represents sexuality, creativity, friendliness, and emotional balance. At an emotional level, this chakra stimulates enthusiasm, hope, and optimism. This chakra also relates to our sense of taste. People who relate easily to others have well-balanced sacral chakras. When the sacral chakra is understimulated we suffer from negative emotions like anger, frustration, and resentment. When it's overstimulated, we are likely to be manipulative, aggressive, and self-indulgent.

Useful stones for the sacral chakra include orange agates, amber, calcite (red or gold), carnelian (red or orange), chalcedony, citrine, golden topaz, red coral, jasper (rainbow or Indian), moonstone, rutilated quartz, and sunstone.

Solar Chakra
Color: Yellow
Element: Fire
Sense: Sight
Desires: To understand
Challenge: To communicate effectively with loved ones
Keyword: Intellect

The solar chakra is situated at the level of the solar plexus, above the navel. It provides us with warmth, happiness, and good self-esteem. When it's working efficiently, this chakra relates to absorption and assimilation of food, providing good digestion and a sense of physical well-being. The solar chakra also relates to our eyes. This isn't surprising. When we're feeling happy and full of the joys of life, everything in the world seems much brighter. This chakra also relates to sensitivity. At an emotional level, this chakra creates optimism, creativity, confidence, and self-respect. Anger and hostility can build up in this chakra when we're living negatively. When the solar chakra is overstimulated we become perfectionists, workaholics, and overly demanding. When it's understimulated we lack confidence and feel a loss of control.

Useful stones for the solar chakra include peach aventurine, yellow carnelian, yellow citrine, red coral, emerald, fluorite, malachite, peridot, rutilated quartz, sunstone, and tiger's eye.

Heart Chakra
Color: Green
Element: Air
Sense: Touch
Desires: To love and be loved
Challenge: To gain confidence
Keyword: Emotions

The heart chakra is in the center of the chest, in line with the heart. It relates to love, friendship, understanding, and the sense of touch. It enables us to give and receive unconditional love and friendship. On the emotional level, this chakra enhances compassion, self-acceptance, and respect for self and others. When this chakra is in balance we're in touch with our feelings and can nurture ourselves as well as others. When this chakra is understimulated, we're over-sensitive and overly sympathetic. We feel timid, afraid, and sorry for ourselves. It's common for co-dependent people to have an understimulated heart chakra. If the chakra is overstimulated we become demanding, possessive, and controlling.

Useful stones for the heart chakra include moss agate, green aventurine, bloodstone, green calcite, chrysoprase, green fluorite, garnet, green jasper, green obsidian, and green tourmaline.

The Trinity

The three top chakras are known as the trinity, or triad. They vibrate at a higher level than the lower four chakras.

Throat Chakra
Color: Blue
Sense: Sound
Desires: Inner peace
Challenge: To risk
Keyword: Concepts

The throat chakra is situated at the level of the throat. It relates to sound, communication, and self-expression. At an emotional level, it enhances idealism, understanding, and love. When the throat chakra is balanced we feel happiness, peace of mind, and contentment. When this chakra is overstimulated we can be arrogant, unbending, sarcastic, overbearing, and conceited. When it's understimulated we become weak, deceitful, and unreliable.

Useful stones for the throat chakra include amazonite, angelite, aquamarine, blue lace agate, blue calcite, chalcedony, chrysocolla, quartz, blue topaz, and turquoise.

Brow Chakra
Color: Indigo
Desires: To be in harmony with the universe
Challenge: To make one's dreams a reality
Keyword: Intuition

The brow chakra is situated in the forehead, between the eyebrows. It is sometimes called the third eye chakra. This chakra governs the mind and influences and controls all the other chakras. Nothing can be created without thought. This is the main function of the brow chakra. At an emotional level, it increases our understanding of life by making us aware of our spiritual natures. Intuition comes from the brow chakra, too. This includes minor examples, such as picking up on someone's feelings and moods. When the brow chakra is overstimulated we become proud, authoritative, calculating, and rigid. When this chakra is understimulated we become unassertive, timid, and nervous.

Useful stones for the brow chakra include amethyst, azurite, clear fluorite, howlite, labradorite, lapis lazuli, moldavite, opal, quartz, and blue sapphire.

Crown Chakra
Color: Violet
Desires: Universal understanding
Challenge: To grow in knowledge and wisdom
Keyword: Spirituality

The crown chakra is situated at the top of the head and controls the strongest energy vibrations in the body. It is often depicted as a halo when artists paint someone who is spiritually evolved. The crown chakra balances the outer and inner sides of our natures. It also governs the spiritual side of our being where we discover our interconnectedness with all living things. When this chakra is overstimulated we become frustrated, disparaging, dejected, and depressed. Migraine headaches are common when this chakra is overstimulated. When the crown chakra is understimulated we become withdrawn, uncommunicative, and lack any pleasure in life.

Useful stones for the crown chakra include alexandrite, amethyst, gold calcite, clear celestite, diamond, clear fluorite, opal, clear quartz, selenite, sugilite, and tourmaline.

Now that you've found your crystal and know how to look after it, it's time to look at some of the different ways you can use it to help others and yourself. Part 2 contains fifty ways to use your crystal.

PART 2

◆

50 WAYS TO USE A CRYSTAL

1: CRYSTAL MEDITATION

Meditation involves relaxing, quieting the mind, and focusing your attention on a specific object or idea. In Eastern forms of meditation this may be a mantra or a sacred word that is repeated constantly to diffuse the mind and empty it of thoughts. In Western meditation, the goal is to relax the mind and use it to focus on one topic to the exclusion of everything else. This topic usually relates to self-development or spiritual growth. Both forms of meditation produce feelings of calmness and inner peace in the mind, body, and spirit that last long after the meditation is over.

Meditation has many health benefits, such as reducing stress, lowering blood pressure, and controlling pain, and can be used as a "[treatment] for a broad range of medical illnesses" (Shonin, Van Gordon, Griffiths 2013).

Meditating with a crystal is especially beneficial, as the crystal helps align the body's energies to provide as much benefit from the meditation as possible.

How to Meditate with Your Crystal

Set aside a time and place where you won't be disturbed for at least thirty minutes. Make sure that the room is pleasantly warm, but not overly hot. Wear loose fitting clothes. If you wish, play some gentle meditation music. Don't play anything that has a tune you recognize. You may like to have a pillow and rug to help you relax.

1. Lie down on your back. I lie on the floor, but you might prefer to lie on a rubber mat or a blanket. (I don't recommend lying on a bed since many people, myself included, fall asleep if they get too comfortable during the meditation.) Bend your knees if you find it hard to relax your lower back. Hold your crystal in your right hand if you're right-handed, or your left hand if you're not.

2. Close your eyes and take three slow, deep breaths, and allow yourself to relax on each exhale.

3. Forget about your breathing and focus on the toes of your left foot, telling them to relax. Stay focused on your toes until you feel them dissolve and let go. Once they feel completely loose, allow these feelings to gradually spread into your foot until your entire foot is relaxed.

4. Allow the relaxation to gradually move into your ankle, and then continue relaxing your calf muscles, knee, and thigh muscles until your entire left leg is totally relaxed.

5. Repeat the process with the toes of your right foot and allow the relaxation to drift all the way up your leg.

6. Continue the process by relaxing your stomach muscles and allowing the pleasant relaxation to drift up to your chest and into both of your shoulders.

7. Allow the relaxation to drift down your left arm to the tips of your fingers. Repeat this process with your right arm.

8. Relax the muscles in your neck, then allow the relaxation to drift into your face and head. Give special attention to the muscles around your eyes. They are the finest muscles in your body. When they relax, your whole body will follow suit.

9. Allow the relaxation to drift up to the top of your head. You should now be completely relaxed throughout your entire body.

10. Mentally scan your body to make sure that every part is as relaxed as it should be. Focus your attention on any areas that are not as relaxed as they should be, and will them to relax.

11. Scan your body again to confirm that you're totally relaxed. If necessary, repeat step 10.

12. Keep your eyes closed and become aware of your slow, rhythmic breathing. You should be breathing through your stomach rather than your chest. Raise the hand that's holding your crystal and move it over the area of your root chakra. The tip of the crystal should be pointing upward and the base should be close to or in contact with your body.

13. Visualize a healing white light entering the tip of your crystal every time you inhale, and allow this healing energy to spread from the base of the crystal into your root chakra when you exhale. You may feel a pleasant sensation of warmth or comfort as you do this. Even if you don't experience this, know that you're stimulating the energy created by the chakra with each breath.

14. Continue holding the crystal over your root chakra for as long as you wish, but for at least a minute. Once you become used to this exercise, you'll find that you'll gradually lengthen the time you hold the crystal over each chakra.

15. When you feel ready, move the crystal over your sacral chakra and repeat the process. Continue doing this until you've energized all seven chakras.

16. When you've finished energizing the chakras, allow the hand that's holding your crystal to lie by your side. Mentally scan your body again and sense what changes have occurred during the meditation.

17. Remain lying in this quiet, meditative state for as long as you wish. When you sense it's time to carry on with your day, take five slow, deep breaths, silently counting them as you do so, and then open your eyes.

18. Continue lying on your back for a minute or two, then get up.

19. As soon as possible after the meditation, have a drink of water and something to eat. Some people feel "spaced out" after a meditation, and eating and drinking helps you return to reality. This is called "grounding."

Once you've become used to this meditation you might choose to enhance it by adding a color and an affirmation to each chakra.

The root chakra relates to red. When you visualize energy coming in through the tip of your crystal, "see" it as red energy. Once you visualize this, say to yourself something along the lines of "I have all the power and energy I need to achieve anything I desire. I am safe and secure." Repeat this affirmation several times.

The sacral chakra relates to orange. Visualize orange energy, while saying something along the lines of "I am healthy, passionate, and full of life. I feel good about my body and my sexuality."

The solar plexus chakra relates to yellow. The affirmation is "I am motivated, powerful, and successful. I accept myself."

The heart chakra relates to green. A suitable affirmation would be: "I am a worthwhile, loving, and compassionate person. I give and receive love."

The throat chakra relates to blue, and the affirmation is: "I am a positive person and I express myself honestly. I express my love to others."

The brow chakra relates to indigo. The affirmation is: "I accept and appreciate the world as it is. I am wise and inspired."

The crown chakra relates to violet. The affirmation is something along the lines of "I am safe and protected, as I'm one with the Divine."

Third Eye Meditation

With this meditation, lie on your back and, before starting, place your crystal between your eyebrows, over your third eye.

Go through stages one to twelve of the first meditation, and then lie quietly and see what comes into your mind. You may experience a fantastical story, or perhaps relive a long-forgotten incident from your past. Enjoy the experience and then count from one to five and return to the present. Remove the crystal and lie quietly for a minute or two before getting up.

When you feel ready, evaluate what occurred to see what lessons you may have learned, and why they are important or relevant to your current life.

This meditation should last no longer than fifteen minutes.

Crystal Focus Meditation

Your crystal is the focal point of this meditation.

Sit down in a straight-backed chair about six feet away from your crystal. Place your feet flat on the ground and rest your hands on your thighs or in your lap.

Stare at the crystal while taking slow, deep breaths. When your eyes start feeling heavy, allow them to close. Focus on your breathing.

Wait to see what comes into your mind, and allow your thoughts to flow freely. You may experience insights on matters that are occurring in your life. You may receive glimpses of the future or memories of the past. You may receive no apparent insights at all. When this occurs, think about what happened in the meditation afterward, as there may be a hidden message that you didn't pick up at the time.

2: GROUNDING YOURSELF

Grounding enables you to release any negative or excess energy from your body. It creates security and helps you feel comfortable in all types of situations.

Do you recall a time when you felt overwhelmed, spaced out, or overly emotional? If you had grounded yourself at that time, you would have been able to let go of the built-up energies. You may have had times when you called on extra energy to do a certain task, such as helping someone who was in pain. Once the task was accomplished it would have been beneficial to let go of any excess energy, enabling you to return to a natural state of balance. Sudden anger or aggression builds up an overload of negative energy that can cause health problems if it's not released. Introverts struggle with feeling overwhelmed more than extroverts do, and grounding is helpful so you can restore your energy levels to whatever is right for you. Grounding enables you to reconnect to the physical world.

With practice, you can ground yourself in a matter of seconds. However, it's better to allow as much time as necessary to enable you to regain your natural state of stability.

Here's an example of a grounding exercise:

1. Stand barefoot outside on grass or earth with your legs slightly apart.

2. Using your left hand, hold your crystal against your skin just above your navel in the area of your third chakra. Place the palm of your right hand against the back of your left hand.

3. Close your eyes and visualize all the stress, tension, and excess energy flowing downward through your body, down your legs, and into the ground through your feet.

4. Visualize it going deep, deep into the ground as it returns to its source.

5. Now that your body has released all the negativity, visualize yourself surrounded by a cocoon of white light. Take several slow, deep breaths. Each time you inhale, you can visualize every cell of your body being stimulated and energized by this pure white light.

6. Sense the white light recharging all your chakras. Feel it reaching into your palms and from there into your crystal.

7. Once you feel completely full of white light, pause and enjoy it for as long as you can.

8. When you feel ready, allow the white light to travel down your legs, through your feet, and into the ground. Visualize it going deep into the earth.

9. Take a deep breath, hold it for a few moments, and open your eyes as you exhale. I like to say "I'm centered and grounded" while holding my breath.

You should feel reinvigorated and relaxed after this exercise. Hold your crystal if you encounter any negativity for the rest of the day, and it will immediately disappear.

Obviously, there'll be times when you'll need to ground yourself instantly. When this occurs, hold the crystal over your solar plexus chakra and visualize a stream of white light descending from the sky and bathing every cell of your body as it passes from your head to your feet and down deep into the ground. The chances are good that you won't be able to stand barefoot on earth or grass. You might even be on the seventh floor of an office building. This doesn't matter. Visualize the energy leaving your feet and flowing all the way down to, and into, the ground.

I prefer to ground myself while standing, but you can also ground yourself while sitting in a chair, or even lying in bed. I know several people who ground themselves every morning before getting out of bed.

Grounding is a useful way of returning you to your normal self after any meditation, visualization, spellwork, or ritual.

Here's a slightly different grounding exercise you can do whenever you need additional strength or confidence. It involves imagining that you're firmly rooted to the ground like a tree.

1. Stand with your feet slightly apart. Hold your crystal by your side in your left hand.

2. Take several slow, deep breaths and allow yourself to relax with each exhalation.

3. Focus on your feet, and then think of the floor beneath your feet, and the ground beneath that.

4. Visualize strong, powerful roots growing from your feet, reaching down to the ground, and then spreading deep into the earth.

5. Allow yourself to feel grounded, empowered, and supremely confident.

This grounding exercise can be expanded by visualizing all the stress and strain in your body traveling down through the roots and dissipating into the earth. Once you've done that, visualize healing energies coming up from the earth, giving you all the strength, power, and encouragement you could ever need.

The Grounding Walk

You can ground yourself whenever you're walking anywhere. I like doing this barefoot in a park, but you can do it anywhere, at any time. Your crystal should be in contact with your skin while you're doing this. The easiest way is to hold it in one hand while you're walking.

As you walk, visualize negative energy leaving your body through your right foot (left foot if you're left-handed) every time it touches the ground. Visualize positive energy entering your body through your left foot (right foot if you're left-handed) each time it contacts the ground.

Experiment by walking slowly and then speeding up, and see if you notice any difference. Continue walking at the pace that works best for you. Even a few paces are beneficial, but it's better to walk for at least twenty minutes, if you can.

Your crystal will benefit from your grounding, too, and you'll find that after a grounding walk, your crystal will keep you grounded for the rest of the day.

There are many ways to ground yourself. Yawning and stretching are effective. Eating a meal is also good, provided you concentrate on what you're doing, rather than watching TV, reading, or chatting with others. Not surprisingly, gardening is one of the best ways to ground yourself. Placing your hands on the ground works well. Spending time on a hobby or doing anything pleasurable is another effective way to ground yourself. Even a good belly laugh is highly beneficial.

3: CENTERING AND BALANCING YOURSELF

As its name suggests, centering yourself means living in harmony with your physical, mental, emotional, and spiritual selves. Your center is not a physical space inside you. It's where every aspect of your being connects with the Universal Life Force. Consequently, when you're centered, you're powerful and have a sense of being in control of your life.

You should feel centered all the time, but if you're like most people, you sometimes pass control to others. You might let someone else make all the decisions, as it avoids disagreements. It might seem easier to accept other people's thoughts and emotions, rather than making your own mind up on whatever it happens to be. When you regain your center, you regain control and take responsibility for your thoughts and actions. You're able to impartially evaluate other people's thoughts, ideas, and beliefs, and make your own mind up about them. When you work from your center you're fully connected and in perfect union with the Divine. Your center is where your true self lives.

It's a simple matter to determine if you're centered. If you're feeling weak, flustered, indecisive, or lacking in confidence, for instance, you're not centered. However, if you're feeling strong, confident, in control, and peaceful, you are.

Here's an exercise you should do whenever you realize you're not centered.

Centering Meditation

Required: one white candle and your crystal.

1. Start the meditation by grounding yourself. Sit
   down comfortably and visualize yourself sending
   roots from the base of your spine deep down into
   the earth. Grounding and centering are often performed together. Grounding enables you to contact
   the earth, while centering enables you to be in touch
   with your innermost self.

2. Light the candle and place it about six feet in front
   of where you're sitting. You should be able to look
   directly into the candle flame without raising or
   lowering your head. Using both hands, hold your
   crystal against your solar plexus chakra.

3. Spend a few minutes relaxing, while focusing on
   your breathing. Inhale through your mouth and exhale through your nose. You might find it helpful to
   make a humming sound each time you exhale.

4. Say to yourself, "I am peaceful and calm." Listen
   to your body to see if it agrees with you. If it does,
   move on to the next step. If it doesn't, repeat
   step three.

5. Say to yourself, "I feel confident and in control of my
   life." Again, listen to your body and see if it agrees.

6. Focus on the strong roots you planted deep in the earth in step one. Take a deep breath and visualize the strength and wisdom of the earth coming up through the roots and spreading into every cell of your body. You can repeat this three or four times if you wish.

7. Allow the roots to withdraw into your body, and sit quietly for a few moments.

8. Hold your crystal in your cupped hands, and say to it, "I am confident and in control of my life." Gaze at your crystal and smile as you feel energy and confidence flowing through your body.

9. Get up, snuff out the candle, and continue with your day.

4: GAINING CLARITY

The word *clarity* means being lucid, coherent, and easily understood. It's a quality that everyone needs. Most people experience times when the future seems foggy and it's hard to decide where to go or what to do. Life is much easier when you know what you want and can express yourself clearly. This is called mental clarity.

Emotional clarity relates to the individual understanding their emotions and knowing why they are experiencing them. Knowing this enables the person to take the actions or make the decisions that are necessary to alleviate the problem.

You can gain mental clarity by ensuring that you have enough sleep, sufficient exercise, and foods that are good for you.

Achieving emotional clarity is not quite as easy, as it uses both your head and your heart. A good way to start is to choose any feeling you're currently experiencing and ask yourself questions about it. Thinking about your feelings helps put them into perspective and sometimes provides solutions.

Fortunately, your crystal can also help you achieve mental and emotional clarity.

1. Decide exactly what you want. You'll achieve better results if you work on one subject at a time. You can't, for instance, ask for the ability to speak easily

in front of others (mental clarity) at the same time that you ask for help in overcoming grief (emotional clarity). Your crystal will help you with both, but you'll achieve better results if you do one at a time. The exception to this is if you ask for more clarity in your life. This is a general request, with no specific questions.

2. Sit down comfortably with your crystal and ask it to help you with your request.

3. Carry the crystal with you and place it where you can see it easily whenever you stop in one place for any length of time. You might, for instance, display your crystal in the kitchen while preparing dinner, and then move it into the dining room when you sit down to eat. At bedtime, you could display your crystal somewhere in the bedroom. At work, you might have the crystal sitting on your desk or somewhere else where you can see it easily.

4. Each time you notice your crystal, silently thank it for helping you achieve your goal. Whenever you find yourself thinking about your concern, touch your crystal for a few seconds and you'll find your tension levels and heart rate will decrease.

5. At least once a day, hold your crystal in your cupped hands and reprogram it. If you're seeking emotional

clarity, finish by holding it against your heart chakra for several seconds. Hold it against your throat chakra for several seconds if you're seeking mental clarity.

Mental Clarity Ritual

This is a helpful ritual that will help you gain mental clarity whenever you need it. Start performing the ritual on the evening of the new moon and repeat it every night until the full moon. This is because between the new and full moon the moon appears to grow. This phenomenon is called a waxing moon. For hundreds of years, magicians have performed rituals during this period when they want something to grow or increase. Rituals involving vanishing or reducing are usually performed from the full moon to the new moon.

Required: one white candle, your crystal, a metal container, pen, paper, and an envelope.

1. Place the candle and crystal on a table in front of you, with the crystal in front of the candle. Place the writing paper and pen in front of these.

2. Light the candle and sit down at the table. You should be able to look directly at the flame of the candle without raising or lowering your head.

3. Think about your need for mental clarity and write a letter to the Universal Life Force saying exactly what you need it for. You should also record the

results that you desire once you've attained the clarity you need. Take as long as you wish, and write down anything that appears relevant. Finish the letter by signing your name. Read the letter, out loud if possible, and seal it in your envelope. Place it in front of the candle and crystal.

4. Pick up your crystal and hold it in your cupped hands. Tell the crystal (silently or out loud) the contents of your letter, and ask it to help you attain your goal. Once you sense that you've received your crystal's agreement, place it on top of the envelope.

5. Gaze into the candle flame and visualize what your life will be like once you've attained the clarity you desire. See it as clearly as you can in your mind's eye. Hold this image in your mind for as long as you can.

6. Raise your crystal and remove the envelope before replacing the crystal. Kiss the envelope and then burn it in the candle flame. As it burns, visualize your request floating up to the Ultimate Light Source, where it will be acted upon. Place the burning envelope into the metal container before it gets too hot to handle.

7. Once the envelope has been completely consumed, say a quiet thank you and snuff out the candle.

8. Repeat the ritual once a day until the full moon. The letter may be different each time you write it. This is good, as it enables you to add any additional information you'd like to send to the architect of the universe.

Your request will usually be fulfilled by the time the full moon arrives. If it doesn't, wait until the next new moon and start performing the ritual again.

5: DEALING WITH REGRETS

There can't be many people out there who have no regrets. Most people have said or done something that they later regret. Everyone makes mistakes. Regrets are often accompanied by feelings of shame, remorse, guilt, embarrassment, and self-condemnation. These feelings can last for years, or even a lifetime.

Regrets can occur in any area of life. Someone might regret not having furthered their education, or maybe not standing up to a bully while in grade school. Many people regret not following their dreams. Recently, I spoke with a man dying from a terminal illness. His regret was that he'd spent too much time at work, at the expense of his home and family life. I regret not staying in contact with friends I made while living in the UK when I was in my early twenties.

If you're endlessly analyzing a regret, you're living in the past. It's bad for your mental health to be crippled in this way. Sometimes it's possible to remedy the situation and apologize. You should do this if you can. It doesn't matter if the person refuses the apology; you've done what you can to rectify the situation. If an apology isn't possible, you should do your best to forgive yourself and let the regret go.

Here's a ritual to help release your regrets:

1. Sit down at a table with pen and paper. Place your crystal on the table on your right-hand side (left if you're left-handed).

2. Think about your regret, and become aware of any feelings this produces.

3. When you feel ready, pick up your pen and write a letter to the person you've hurt. This could be the younger you if your regret relates to an action or inaction, rather than a person. No one will read this letter, so you can write down whatever you wish. You're likely to experience a variety of emotions as you do this. Allow yourself to shout, cry, or do anything else that helps you release these pent-up emotions. Finish the letter by apologizing for your actions (or inactions) and sign it.

4. Read the letter and think about any lessons you've learned from the experience.

5. Fold the letter and seal it in an envelope. Write the name of the person you wrote the letter to on the front. Place the letter on the table and lay your crystal on it.

6. Look at the letter and say, preferably out loud: "No one is perfect. I'm not perfect, but I'm owning up to my mistakes and I forgive myself." Repeat these words twice.

7. Go outdoors and set fire to the envelope. Hold the crystal in the smoke produced by the burning letter.

8. When the contents of your letter have been sent out to the universe, hold your crystal and squeeze it slightly as you say, "I forgive myself."

9. As soon as possible after burning the envelope and letter, enjoy a restful, relaxing bath. Use bath salts or a tablespoon of salt. This is a reward for what you've done, and it also helps eliminate any residual negativity that might be stored in your body. When you get out of the bath, watch the water go down the drain, and realize that the negativity is being washed away with the water. Have a shower if a bath is not available.

10. Send positive thoughts of love and success to the person you wrote the letter to. Wish that person a long, healthy, and happy life. Visualize the person receiving your thoughts and smiling at you.

As you've held onto this regret for a long time, you may need to repeat this ritual until you feel you've completely forgiven yourself.

6: HANDLING GRIEF

Grief is a natural response to losing someone who has been close to you. Everyone grieves in their own way, and it takes time for life to gain some semblance of normality again. Eventually you'll come to accept your loss, but you'll never forget it, as your memories will remain with you forever.

Your crystal can help you handle the different stages of grief and ultimately bring you to a state of acceptance.

One of the simplest, yet most effective ways to handle your grief over the loss of a special person is to sit outside with your crystal in your hands and think about them. Remember the times you spent together and the different things you did. Smile at the happy memories and allow yourself to weep while reliving some of the sad times. Squeeze your crystal and tell this special person that you'll always keep them in your heart.

Solo Grief Ritual

This is a ritual that you can adapt to suit your circumstances. All you need is a white candle, a small table, and your crystal. If you find it hard to kneel for any length of time, you'll also need a straight-backed chair.

1. Create a circle at least nine feet in diameter to perform the ritual in. You can mark the circle in any way you wish. A friend of mine uses cards from her tarot deck to indicate the circumference. Another person

I know uses pebbles and small ornaments. I usually
use a circular rug I bought especially for performing rituals on. Before I had it, I used a length of rope
to create a circle. Mark the four cardinal directions:
north, south, east, and west.

2. Place the table in the middle of your circle and put
   the candle and your crystal on it.

3. Leave the circle once you've completed these prepa-
   rations. You can reenter the circle whenever you
   wish. I usually wait about five minutes, and spend
   that time slowly drinking a glass of water and thinking about the ritual.

4. When you're ready, enter the circle. Light the candle
   and face east. Visualize Archangel Raphael standing
   outside the circle, guarding and protecting the eastern quadrant. You can picture the archangels in any
   way you wish. I see Raphael as a traveler carrying a
   staff and a fish. Thank him for his protection.

5. Turn ninety degrees and face south. Visualize Archangel Michael protecting the south quadrant. Thank
   him for protecting you during the ritual. I picture
   Archangel Michael as a soldier wearing chainmail,
   holding a sword, and resting one foot on a dragon.

6. Turn to face west and visualize Archangel Gabriel protecting the western quadrant. Thank Gabriel for providing protection. I visualize Archangel Gabriel in blue robes, carrying a trumpet.

7. Face north and visualize Archangel Uriel protecting the northern quadrant. Thank him for his help and protection. I see Archangel Uriel wearing brown robes and carrying a scroll.

8. Kneel in front of the table, pick up your crystal, and fondle it as you gaze into the light of the candle. Think about the person you are grieving for, and allow memories of them to pass through your mind.

9. When you feel ready, speak to this person. Say all the things you wish you had said while they were alive. Thank your friend for all the love and friendship you shared. Mention some of the special times you had together. Finish by saying that you're letting them go now, but they will remain forever in your heart. Kiss your crystal and snuff out the candle.

10. Stand up and face east. Thank Archangel Raphael for protecting you, and for watching over you while you were conducting the ritual. Continue by facing south and thanking Archangel Michael, followed by Gabriel and Uriel.

11. Carry the crystal with you. Whenever you feel sad about your loss, fondle the crystal. This will now help you think happy thoughts about your friend.

This ritual will provide healing for you. You can repeat it if you wish, but at some stage you need to let them go, so that you are able to get on with your own life.

7: DEALING WITH THE ENEMY WITHIN

We all have an enemy inside of us, a negative voice that criticizes and judges us. The enemy within blames us for failing to reach impossibly difficult demands and compares us unfavorably to others. It exaggerates our weaknesses and constantly tries to put us down. It undermines our accomplishments and tells us we're not good enough. No matter how hard we try, it's impossible to satisfy the enemy within.

We're all effectively divided inside. Part of us is goal-oriented and forward-looking, while the other half is self-critical and fearful. We can feel positive and happy one second, and a moment later feel dejected and despondent. A common example is feeling happy and then seeing yourself in a mirror and thinking, "I'm ugly. Look how fat I am. How could anyone like me?"

Because it's always been there, we usually take this inner voice for granted, and unthinkingly accept what it tells us. Therefore, we undermine ourselves by thinking thoughts along the lines of "I'm so stupid," "I'm a failure," "I'm useless," or "I never succeed in relationships." Imagine a young man's chance of getting a date if he said to himself, "She's out of my league. She'll never go out with me," as he was being introduced to her. His thoughts automatically drained him of confidence, and chances are he'd make a poor impression.

It can be an interesting experiment to listen carefully to your enemy within for one full day. If possible, write your thoughts down. Count the number of negative, harmful, and critical comments it makes. You're likely to be surprised at the number of times you're being belittled by this negative part of your nature during a single day.

Fortunately, with the help of your crystal, you can overrule the enemy within and become the person you want to be. Here are some suggestions for how to do this:

- Instill your crystal with positive affirmations that show your true worth.

- Give the enemy within a name. Give it the weakest, funniest name you can. Every time you address it by name, you'll realize what a pathetic weakling it is.

- Make a list of situations in which you know your enemy within may try to undermine you.

- Carry your crystal with you. Whenever you hear your enemy within attempt to put you down, touch or hold your crystal and silently say, "I've had enough of you. Stop!" Pause for a second or two and then add, "I'm worthy of the very best that life has to offer."

- Before entering a situation where you know your enemy within will attack you, hold your crystal and tell yourself that you are intelligent, confident, and in complete control.

- With the help of your crystal and your affirmation, chances are your enemy within will remain quiet. However, if it decides to speak negatively tell it to stop! Again, wait a second or two and say, "I'm worthy of the very best that life has to offer."

- Continue doing this for at least a month. At the same time, continue bolstering yourself with positive affirmations. Keep telling yourself that you're a positive person. Deliberately place yourself in some of the situations you wrote down earlier, and enjoy telling your enemy within to stop if it dares to appear.

- Be particularly careful of your enemy within if you're feeling sad, anxious, depressed, or overtired. At these times it will try to take over your life, and you need to be prepared to tell it where to go if it makes an appearance.

- Your enemy within can appear at any time. Sooner or later, it will show up when you least expect it. When this happens, touch or hold your crystal, and tell it where to go. Say a positive affirmation (silently or out loud), tell yourself you're a worthwhile person, and carry on, free of the negativity created by your enemy within.

- You might like to play a game with your enemy within. Every time it suggests something, do the opposite. If it says, "You can't do that. If you try, you'll fail," laugh, and prove your enemy within wrong.

Realize that you won't be able to eliminate the enemy within from your life. However, you can neutralize it and that is just as good, especially when you find how enjoyable it is to tell it to stop.

8: FORGIVING YOURSELF AND OTHERS

Forgiving yourself and others is one of the most liberating things you can do. It enables you to let go of the past and start moving forward again. Holding onto grudges, resentment, anger, pain, negativity, and thoughts of revenge damages you mentally and emotionally. There's even some evidence that doing this can affect you physically as well. As you forgive yourself and others, you release these negative thoughts and emotions and start living again. You'll become a more open and positive person, and will enjoy better relationships with everyone you interact with. Because of this, it's vital for your future happiness that you learn how to forgive.

When you forgive someone, you're not letting the person get away with whatever it was they did. You're not forgetting whatever it was that happened. You're not condoning their actions.

What you *are* doing is setting yourself free. The same thing applies with forgiving yourself. Everyone makes mistakes, but hanging onto them and making yourself miserable helps no one. Forgive yourself and set yourself free.

It's not easy to forgive someone when you've been badly hurt. Your crystal can give you the necessary strength and courage to forgive and let go.

Heart Chakra Ritual

This ritual can be used to forgive yourself and as many other people as you wish. Before the ritual, enjoy a pleasant bath and put on some loose-fitting clothes. Choose somewhere warm where you can lie down for about twenty minutes. I always lie on the floor, as I tend to fall asleep when performing rituals in bed.

1. Lie down comfortably and place your crystal over your heart.

2. Take several slow, deep breaths and then gradually relax every part of your body. I start with the toes of my left foot and gradually relax every muscle in my left leg. I repeat this with my right leg, and then relax my body, shoulders, left arm and hand, right arm and hand, neck, and head.

3. Think in general terms about the person or persons you're forgiving in this ritual. Include yourself, if you're forgiving yourself. Think about what each person has done to hurt you, but try to be as dispassionate as possible. If you start feeling emotional, immediately start thinking about something else. I like to imagine myself lying beside a small stream. In my imagination, I place any thoughts or emotions I don't want onto a leaf that I place in the water where I can watch the stream carry it away.

4. Once you've thought about everyone you wish to forgive, visualize yourself lying wherever you happen to be and "see" your body turning into a large ball of wool. There are strands of wool leading off in all directions. These strands are all the negative thoughts and emotions you've been hanging on to. Smile and think about how good your life will be once you've eliminated all this unnecessary stress from your life.

5. In your imagination, see a giant pair of scissors and watch as it cuts off every strand of wool that you no longer need. Continue watching until the ball of wool is perfect and round, with no strands leading away from it.

6. Allow your heart chakra to fill with happiness and joy now that you're free of the chains that have been holding you back. Feel that joy and happiness moving into your crystal, filling it with love and freedom. Focus on your heart chakra for as long as you can.

7. When you feel ready, thank yourself for what you've achieved. Thank the Universal Life Force for helping you feel whole again.

8. Count slowly from one to five and open your eyes.

You should feel a strong sense of pride and joy when you get up. Repeat this ritual every few days until all the strands of wool have disappeared, and you see nothing but a round, smooth ball of wool.

Keep your crystal with you and touch or handle it several times a day. Whenever you do this, say to yourself: "I'm free. I've let go of the past and am moving forward again. I forgive myself, and I forgive everyone who has hurt me." Give your crystal a squeeze and continue with your day.

Two Chairs Ritual

You can use this ritual to forgive one person at a time. You'll need two straight-backed chairs. Place them facing each other in the center of a room, about six feet apart. Place your crystal on the floor halfway between the two chairs.

1. Sit down in one of the chairs and close your eyes. Take several slow, deep breaths and imagine a steady stream of pure, white, healing light descending from the sky, passing through the roof and other parts of the building you're in, and gradually filling up the room you're in with Divine healing energy.

2. Inhale the healing energy and let it filter through you, healing and energizing every cell of your body.

3. In your mind's eye, visualize the person you're planning to forgive sitting in the chair facing you. They are also receiving the benefit of the pure white light.

4. Tell this person that you forgive them for all the hurt, grief, and anguish their comments or actions caused you. Sometimes this will start a conversation in your mind. If this happens, allow the conversation to continue for as long as you wish. You may be surprised at what the person tells you.

5. Open your eyes, pick up the crystal, and place it on the other person's chair. Sit down again, close your eyes, and say something along the lines of "My crystal sends out light, love, and everything that's good in the universe. Now that I've forgiven you, I want you to have your share of all the goodness the world provides, as we are one."

6. Visualize the person receiving positive energy from your crystal. Sit quietly in peace and harmony with the person you visualized on the other chair, the person you've forgiven.

7. Open your eyes and take back the crystal. Hold it in your cupped hands as you complete the ritual.

8. Give thanks to the Universal Life Force for helping you to let go and forgive.

Repeat this ritual as often as necessary until you've completely forgiven the person.

9: RESOLVING NEGATIVE ENERGY

Negative emotions are reflected in the body. If they're not dealt with, they can cause mental and physical problems. Everyone has negative thoughts from time to time, but they have little long-term effect if they're balanced by an equal number of positive thoughts.

Unfortunately, many people are their own worst enemy, as they endlessly focus on their fears, worries, doubts, and other concerns. They spend more time thinking about the bad things that they believe have been done to them than the good things that have happened in their lives.

Here's a ritual that can help people suffering from a negative outlook realize how many positive qualities they have and stop overthinking the negativity in their lives.

Required: pen, paper, envelope, and your crystal.

1. Place the paper on a table and sit down in front of it. Place the crystal beside the sheet of paper.

2. Write down as many positive qualities about yourself that you can. Take all the time you need.

3. When you've finished, fold up the sheet of paper and seal it inside of the envelope. Place the envelope on the table in front of you.

4. Pick up your crystal and hold it for a few seconds before placing it on the envelope.

5. In your imagination, visualize your crystal absorbing all your positive traits from the sheet of paper inside the envelope. Focus on this for at least two minutes.

6. Pick up the crystal and thank it for shielding you from any negativity and for filling you with unlimited positive energy.

7. Carry the envelope and your crystal with you. Repeat steps 3 to 5 every evening until you feel you no longer need it. When you think of additional positive qualities, write them down and repeat the entire ritual.

How to Remove External Negativity

Negativity is not always self-inflicted. Unfair criticism, idle gossip, insensitive comments, workplace bullying, and people who dislike you for some unknown reason are all examples of external negativity. Rude drivers, bad service, and discourtesy are examples of external negativity from strangers. When you're experiencing these situations, you may feel that everyone is conspiring against you. Everyone experiences external negativity, but you may not realize this since most people don't show it.

There are many ways to deal with external negativity. A common method is to respond to rudeness with rudeness, but that's not a useful solution as it's likely to aggravate the situation. You could let yourself feel small and simply try to deal with the negativity that's being sent to you. You could remove yourself from the situation. This might involve changing jobs or even location. It's an extreme solution, but it could work. Another method is to refuse to let anyone see that you're being affected by the negativity. Act as confidently as you can and ignore the bad behavior of others.

You could also use your crystal to repel any negativity that was directed at you with this ritual:

1. Stand, facing east, holding your crystal with the thumb and first finger of each hand at chest height. Say something along the lines of "I dedicate this crystal to repel any form of negativity that is directed at me. I ask the guardians of the east to help my crystal achieve this." Gaze toward the east and nod your head when you feel you've received an answer.

2. Repeat the same words and actions while facing south, west, and north. Then turn to face east again.

3. Raise your crystal to face height and say a sincere "thank you" to the guardians of the east. Lower your crystal to chest height again, and turn to the south. Repeat this step while facing each direction.

4. Your crystal is now armed and dedicated to repelling any negativity that comes your way.

5. Depending on the volume and strength of the negativity, you might like to perform this ritual every day until you feel you're in control of the situation. When you reach this stage, perform the ritual every few days, and then once a week for as long as necessary.

10: WORKING THROUGH ANGER

Anger is a perfectly natural and normal emotional state that can range from feelings of irritation to a blinding, potentially damaging rage. It's a message that tells you that something is upsetting or threatening you. Consequently, it's natural to feel angry if you've been treated unfairly or have been wronged. If you can't do what you want to do or can't get what you want, it's natural to become frustrated and annoyed.

Many people claim that when they get angry the situation is totally out of their hands. This isn't true. Anyone who wants to can learn how to express their feelings without upsetting or hurting others. Fortunately, a crystal can be a useful way to calm yourself down in a difficult situation, and can help you look at the problem in a peaceful state of mind.

Anger is always accompanied by physiological and biological changes in the body, such as increased heart rate, blood pressure, and adrenaline levels. It also affects the root and solar chakras. People who are frequently angry put themselves at risk of heart disease, high blood pressure, and a range of stress-related health problems.

The natural response to anger is aggression. However, that can lead to even greater problems, which is why we need to learn to handle our angry feelings in a more constructive way. We can, for instance, express our feelings in an assertive way, rather than an aggressive way. This lets everyone who's involved know what our needs are and why we're angry.

Another solution is to deliberately calm down. When I was a child, I was told to take ten slow, deep breaths before speaking whenever I was angry. It's good advice, as it provides time to think, and gives your heart rate an opportunity to slow down. I must confess that I haven't always remembered that advice.

A friend of mine removes himself from the situation when he feels angry, and goes for a brisk walk or does some exercise. This gives him time to calm down and think about the situation before returning to deal with it.

I find it helpful to breathe from the diaphragm while silently repeating "I'm peaceful and calm." Someone I used to work with many years ago would watch the second hand of his watch make two revolutions before deciding how he'd handle a difficult situation.

Unfortunately, there are times when we react too quickly and fail to focus on our breathing or say a peaceful affirmation. It's times like these when a crystal can be extremely helpful.

Imagine how different your life would be if you could immediately calm yourself down in any type of situation. This isn't impossible. You can do this by simply touching your crystal whenever you find yourself in any type of situation that has the potential to make you angry.

The first stage is to program your crystal to make you peaceful and calm whenever you touch it:

1. Start by cleansing your crystal to eliminate any negativity it may have picked up.

2. Sit down comfortably with your crystal in your cupped hands. Take several slow, deep breaths, and then talk to your crystal. Tell it about times in the past when you've failed to keep control of your temper. Tell it how this made you feel, and the effect it had on the other people involved. Tell your crystal that you don't want any repeats of this sort of behavior and that you're asking it to help you feel calm and in total control in every type of situation. Finally, ask, "Will you help me to act appropriately in any situation that may cause me to become angry?"

3. Wait for a response. It may come as a feeling or a sense of knowing that your crystal will help. You may even sense your crystal saying yes. Your crystal may seem warmer or cooler in your hands. Be patient. Wait quietly and it will come.

4. Once you've received a reply, silently thank your crystal, and using both hands, hold it against your heart chakra. Visualize your crystal absorbing peaceful green energy from the chakra. At the same time, it's also receiving all the qualities of love, friendship, peace, and harmony. Hold this visualization for as long as you can.

5. In your mind's eye, "see" your crystal imparting all these good qualities to you whenever you need them. All you need do is touch your crystal and you'll immediately feel peaceful and calm. Naturally, you'll do this when you're feeling angry, but there are many other situations when it would be beneficial to touch your crystal. You might be feeling grumpy, irritable, or out of sorts. You might be tempted to say something hurtful or unkind. You might be kept waiting for an unusually long time when making a phone call. You might be dealing with someone who isn't remotely interested in what you want. You might encounter someone who happens to be in a bad mood. You should also touch your crystal before going into a potentially difficult meeting. Maybe someone doesn't show you the respect you think you deserve. What do you do if someone cuts you off in traffic? These situations and many more will be easier to handle if you touch your crystal.

6. When using your crystal to help you control anger, cleanse it every night to remove the negativity it will have picked up during the day. Be sure to thank your crystal while cleansing it, and again each time you touch it during the day.

A friend of mine uses this technique to control anger. He is sensitive and easily hurt. Unfortunately, he tends to over-react whenever he gets upset. Once he started carrying a crystal to help him handle the stresses and strains of his everyday life, he quickly became calmer and more relaxed. He told me that when he touches his crystal he visualizes green energy coming from it and surrounding him with feelings of warmth and love. "How can I be angry when I love the people I'm interacting with?" he told me.

Over the years, I've shown this technique to many people and they've all had good results. I'm sure it will work just as well for you.

11: CONTROLLING STRESS

There are two types of stress: di-stress and eu-stress. Both forms of stress have a profound effect upon the mind and the body. Di-stress (i.e., distress) is created when the pressures of life become too hard to handle and the person suffers physically and mentally as a result. Common symptoms are headaches, skin problems, lower back pain, and bowel disorders. Di-stress is a major factor in heart disease, too. Eu-stress (i.e., beneficial stress) is a positive form of stress that is caused when the person finds a task stimulating, rather than overwhelming. This person might be grossly overworked, but derives pleasure and satisfaction from whatever they are doing.

Many years ago, someone told me that the only people who don't suffer from stress are in graveyards. Stress is a fact of life, and everyone experiences it from time to time. Problems occur when di-stress is ongoing. Financial pressures, relationship problems, and the drive to succeed in a career are all common causes of stress, and many people suffer from all of them.

Here are two meditations you can perform with your crystal that will help you release unwanted stress.

The Well of Joy

1. Sit down on a comfortable chair with your feet flat on the floor and your hands holding your crystal and resting in your lap.

2. Close your eyes and breathe slowly and deeply. Each time you exhale, say to yourself, "relax, relax, relax." Continue doing this until you feel pleasantly relaxed and comfortable.

3. When you feel totally relaxed, imagine you're enjoying a walk in the country. You have a water bottle in your hand and a rucksack on your back. You're walking along a country lane, and when you turn a corner you see a beautiful, old home. It appears to be unoccupied, and you walk up the driveway into a beautiful courtyard surrounded by rose bushes. In the center is what appears to be a wishing well made from old bricks. It has a wooden roof, with a bucket attached to a rope suspended from it. You walk over and gaze into the well. You can't see the bottom, so you pick up a pebble and drop it in. It takes a few seconds before you hear it land in the water. You look around at the beautiful setting and enjoy the incredible peace and quiet of this place. You think about how wonderful it would be to live in an environment like this, totally free of the stresses you endure in your everyday life.

   For a few moments, think about the major stresses in your life. What would it feel like to drop them into the well? You take off the rucksack and look inside. You're amazed to find that it contains all the stresses, pressures, and other baggage that you've collected. You can't believe that you've been carrying them around with you for so long. You take out a small parcel of stress and drop it into the well. You feel a sense of lightness and relief as you do this. You do it again and again, until the rucksack is empty. You roll your shoulders, stretch, and walk around the well. You feel lighter and enjoy being at peace with yourself. You lean over the well and say thank you. You smile as you continue your walk. Walk for as long as you wish, and when you feel ready, count slowly from one to five and open your eyes.

4. Hold your crystal between the palms of your hands and silently tell it how happy you are to be free of all the stresses that have been holding you back and preventing you from fully enjoying life. Thank it for helping you learn how to control your stress levels.

5. Hold or touch your crystal whenever you find yourself in a potentially stressful situation, and remind yourself that you are free from stress.

6. Repeat this visualization as often as you can. With practice, you'll be able to "see" the well almost as soon as you close your eyes, and will be able to instantly discard any stress you happen to be carrying.

Peaceful Stream

This visualization is similar to the Well of Joy. The major difference is step 3. Start with steps 1 and 2 from the previous meditation. Instead of walking in the countryside, in step 3, visualize yourself in this scene:

Picture yourself sitting under a tree beside a small stream. It's a pleasant, sunny summer's day and you're enjoying the sounds of the running water in the crystal-clear stream. A solitary cloud is floating across the clear, blue sky, and you can hear birds singing in the distance. A gentle breeze caresses your cheek. You think about how perfect this scene would be if you could somehow be free of stress. As you think about the problems in your life, a leaf drops from the tree you're leaning against and lands in your lap. You pick it up and notice that its edges are slightly curved, making it look like a tiny boat. You think how wonderful it would be if you could put all your problems onto this tiny boat and let the stream carry them away from you, ensuring that they could never bother you again. You smile as you decide to do exactly that. You lean over the stream and gently release the boat. You watch your little boat gather speed as it's picked up by the current. You silently thank it as you watch it carry all your problems away. Soon it is out of sight, and you sit under the tree again feeling happier and freer than you've felt for a long, long time. Enjoy your spot beside the stream for as long as you wish. When you feel ready, count from one to five and open your eyes.

Finish the visualization with steps 4 to 6 from the previous meditation.

I've found both visualizations effective for handling stress and have used them with clients as well as myself. In my work as a hypnotherapist, I originally used these visualizations on their own, but started giving each client a small gemstone when I found how much more effective the visualizations were with the addition of a crystal or gemstone.

12: ADDICTIONS AND YOUR CRYSTAL

Addiction occurs when someone becomes compulsively absorbed in an activity that appears pleasurable but has an adverse effect. When people think of addictions, the first things that come to mind are nicotine, alcohol, and other drugs. These are called substance dependence addictions.

The other form of addiction is behavioral dependence addiction. This includes addictions to gambling, shopping, pornography, sex, exercise, and the internet. When people become addicted to something, they lose control, and their craving for whatever it happens to be takes over. It's as if they enter a trance state that lasts until they've satisfied the urge, run out of time, or spent all their available money.

Many people partake in these activities or behaviors, but never become addicted. This is because they have non-addictive personalities. They may find it hard to understand people who become heavily addicted. "I decided not to have another cigarette," they might say. "Why don't you do the same?" Of course, this is extremely difficult for anyone suffering from an addiction.

The fact that someone's become addicted to something is not a sign of a weakness in their character. Experts argue whether an addiction is a mental illness. It's certainly a chemical imbalance. Addicts who seek help need to be supported rather than condemned.

Your crystal can help you overcome an addiction. However, with serious addictions, you'll need medical or other professional help as well as your crystal. There are support groups for all the major addictions. Alcoholics Anonymous, Crystal Meth Anonymous, Co-Dependents Anonymous, and Gamblers Anonymous are all good examples of groups that can provide help, advice, and support.

The following are two crystal rituals that can help in your journey to overcome addiction.

Chakra Ritual for Addiction

1. Sit or lie down comfortably in a warm room, and focus on your breathing until you feel fully relaxed.

2. Hold your crystal in both hands and say, preferably out loud, something along the lines of "My addiction is ruining my life, and I'm determined to free myself from it. I'm prepared to do anything that's necessary to eliminate (whatever it happens to be) from my life. I've made my mind up, and am committed to this goal." (This is the most important part of the ritual. If you're not committed to overcoming your addiction, there's no point in performing it.)

3. Hold your crystal over your root chakra for at least two minutes. Ask your crystal to balance the chakra to help you become free of your addiction.

4. Repeat this with your sacral chakra.

5. Slowly move your crystal up your body, holding it over each chakra in turn.

6. Hold the crystal for at least two minutes over your crown chakra while thanking it for helping you eliminate something that you don't want or need in your life. (The root, sacral, and crown chakras are the most important chakras for this ritual.)

7. Hold your crystal over your root, sacral, and crown chakras again while thanking them for their help in resolving your problem.

8. Hold your crystal in both hands and picture yourself in the near future, leading a life of happiness and joy, totally free of your addiction. See yourself enjoying happy times with the people you love and spending time doing other things you enjoy. Visualize this as clearly as you can, and allow the feelings of happiness and joy to flow into every part of your body.

9. When you feel ready, get up and carry on with your day. If you're doing this in bed at night, roll over and allow yourself to drift into sleep.

Repeat this ritual every day, if possible. Carry your crystal everywhere with you, and touch or hold it whenever you experience an urge to go back to your old way of life. While touching the crystal, remind yourself of the commitment you made to rid yourself of your addiction.

Crystal Rope Spell

Required: a nine-foot length of rope and your crystal.

You need to tie nine knots in your length of rope. While tying them, think of your addiction and the harm it is doing to your life. Tie nine knots on the rope, all evenly spaced apart. Start with knots at each end of the rope, followed by the center knot. Then tie knots between these until you have nine in total.

Look at the knots. These all symbolize your addiction and the fact that you're bound to it.

You might find it helpful to mark the end where you tied your first knot. For the next nine days, you're going to release one knot every day, and you should aim to untie them in the same order that you tied them in.

Try to untie the knots at the same time each day. As you release the knot, imagine that you're also releasing your addiction, more and more every day. Many people like to shout out, "Yes!" or "I'm free!" as they release the knot.

Display the rope where you can see it several times a day. Place your crystal beside the next knot to be untied. Each time you untie a knot, pick up your crystal and fondle it while congratulating yourself on your progress in freeing (untying) yourself from your addiction.

You can repeat this spell as many times as you wish, until your addiction is firmly in the past.

13: ENHANCING YOUR LIFE

Crystals can enhance your life in many ways. The sight of a beautiful crystal is enough to lift most people's spirits. Handling or looking at a favorite crystal helps create peace and calm, no matter how stressful your life might be at the time. Sleeping with your crystal under your pillow can provide peaceful, happy dreams. Placing your crystal where you can see it frequently during the day provides feelings of well-being and happiness.

Here's an exercise you can use to enhance any area of your life that needs additional help. The preparation takes time, but is an enjoyable part of the process. First, make a list of the most important areas of your life. Some may be obvious, such as love, family, and career, but there are others like community, integrity, and purpose that you might want to include. Here are some other possibilities: spirituality, education, friends, social life, health, fitness, hobbies, home, partner, children, money, character, emotions, habits, and quality of life. You don't need all of these these for the purposes of this exercise. Pick the ones that are most important to you—seven to ten should be enough.

Arrange the areas in a list, with the area that's currently providing the greatest level of satisfaction in your life at the top, and the area of least satisfaction at the bottom.

Collect objects that relate to all the areas on your list. You might use a photograph of you and your partner to indicate love, for instance. If you're currently looking for a partner, you might draw a picture of a heart and use that. The objects can be any size you wish. I know someone who has a collection of miniature objects that relate to most areas of life. This means she can perform the ritual on a small coffee table. I usually choose larger objects, such as photographs, drawings, or words constructed from Scrabble tiles, and place them on the floor.

Then follow these steps:

1. Start by arranging the objects in a circle. I like to place the object that needs to be enhanced (the last item on your list) facing east, and then place three more objects in the south, west, and north positions. I then create a circle using the remaining objects. You can create the circle in any way you wish. I always use east as my starting position, but you should use any direction that makes sense to you.

2. If your circle is on the floor, hold your crystal in your cupped hands and walk around the circle three times. Then step inside the circle. If your circle is relatively small, trace around it three times using the forefinger of your right hand while holding your crystal in your left hand.

3. Place the crystal on or in front of the area of your life that needs to be enhanced.

4. Close your eyes and think about this area of your life and what you would like to do to enhance it. Here are some examples: If the area relates to learning, you might decide to read three books a month, or take a course or workshop online, or an evening class. If the area relates to your social life, you might decide to contact at least two friends every week and arrange a dinner or get-together in the next two weeks. If it relates to a vacation, decide where and when you want to go. If it relates to physical fitness, you might commit to going to the gym at least three times every week. If it relates to money, you could think of ways to earn additional money, or decide on things you could do to make you more valuable to your current employer.

5. Pick up your crystal and face in the direction of the area you're enhancing. Say an affirmation, preferably out loud. If it relates to a vacation, you might say: "I am going to (location) for x days in (month you've decided on)." You can include as much additional information as you wish. You might stipulate a particular hotel, and the amount of spending money you'll take with you, for instance. Once you've said your affirmation, squeeze your crystal and say, "I affirm this."

6. Turn ninety degrees clockwise. If you started at the east, turn to face south. Repeat the affirmation, squeeze your crystal, and say, "I affirm this."

7. Do this twice more, and then turn to face the direction you started in.

8. Hold your crystal in your left hand and place the palm of your right hand on top of it. Look at the object that indicates the area you want enhanced, and say something along the lines of "My life will be enhanced when I (whatever it happens to be). With the help of my crystal, I'm starting work on this project today."

9. Place your crystal in the center of your circle. Say a sincere thank you to the Universal Life Force for enhancing your life, and step out of the circle.

The ritual is over, and you can carry on with your day. If possible, leave the circle in place for an hour or two before dismantling it. Repeat this ritual regularly, until you've achieved whatever it is you asked for. Carry your crystal with you and affirm your goal whenever you see or feel it.

Once you've achieved this goal, you can perform the ritual for a different area of your life.

Gratitude Ritual

We all take many areas of our lives for granted. This brief ritual can be done every day, if you wish, to give thanks for all the blessings in your life.

1. Make a list of five to ten things you're grateful for.

2. Hold your crystal in your cupped hands and say, "Thank you (God, Divine Spirit, Architect of the Universe, Universal Life Force, or whatever name you prefer) for all the blessings you have given me that enhance my life. I am especially grateful for (read out the list you wrote). Thank you. Thank you. Thank you."

3. Close your eyes and gently fondle your crystal as you think about the blessings you have in your life. Continue doing this for as long as you can. When your attention starts to wander, count silently from one to five, open your eyes, and carry on with your day.

Here is a slightly different version of the gratitude ritual. Make a list of ten to twenty small activities that you enjoy doing. You are going to do one of these activities every day.

1. On the evening before the first day, decide what activity you're going to do the following day.

2. Close your eyes, hold your crystal in your cupped hands, and say, "Thank you, Divine Spirit, for

enhancing my life in so many ways. Tomorrow I'm
going to (have coffee with a friend, read a book
for twenty minutes, or whatever it happens to be).
Thank you for making this possible. Thank you.
Thank you. Thank you."

3. Gently fondle your crystal as you think about what
you're going to do on the following day.

4. When you feel ready, count from one to five and
open your eyes.

Make sure that you do this activity on the following day.
Once you've done it, choose another activity from your
list. When you perform the ritual again, start by thanking
Divine Spirit (by whatever name you choose) for the activity you did that day, and give thanks in advance for the
activity you'll be doing on the following day.

Once you've worked your way through your list, you
can go through the list again, or create a new list. It's amazing how much a special activity can enhance your life, and
it makes no difference if it's small or large.

14: CRYSTAL PROTECTION

Everyone needs psychic protection, as we've all felt physically, mentally, and emotionally drained at different times in our lives. We've all also experienced stress, pressure, and antagonism. We're affected by negativity in many forms, including the daily news. Some people are extremely sensitive to the moods and feelings of others, and this makes them particularly sensitive to both intentional and unintentional psychic attacks.

Consequently, we all need some form of psychic protection to enable us to function well in everyday life. There are many ways to protect yourself psychically, and one of the most effective methods uses a crystal or gemstone.

People have used crystals and gemstones for protection purposes for thousands of years. The mummy of a young noble woman who died some 3,500 years ago was found at Shêch Abd el-Qurna in Egypt. Her body was adorned with jewelry, including a large necklace that was worn for protection purposes (Kunz 1913, 36).

Salt has been used for purification and protection purposes for thousands of years. A pinch of salt in a cradle, for instance, would protect the baby until it was baptized. Even today, many people sprinkle salt in the four corners of a room to provide protection and a harmonious environment for the occupants. Salt is also sometimes added to a bath to provide protection for the person bathing. It also removes all the negativity that has become attached to the person during the day. A pinch of salt placed under the sheets provides protection for anyone who sleeps in the bed. Because it is so versatile, salt may well be the most important crystal of all, for psychic protection.

For overall protection and well-being, the most effective remedy is to wear a crystal or gemstone that has been dedicated to the task. The easiest way to use it is to wear it as a pendant around your neck. You can display it, if you wish, or wear it underneath your clothes. You can also carry a suitable crystal around with you in a pocket or purse. If possible, take it out and display it somewhere you'll see it frequently during the day. Touch or rub your crystal whenever you experience any form of negativity. This negativity can even come from inside yourself. Touch your crystal whenever you lack confidence, experience doubt or unworthiness, or find yourself thinking negative thoughts.

Circle of Protection

A circle of protection is an invisible shield that you can place around yourself whenever you find yourself in a difficult or stressful situation. Any stress that comes at you will be deflected away by the shield, leaving you calm and relaxed inside. In fact, the more stress there is outside, the more relaxed you'll feel inside. If you wish, you can visualize the stress hitting the shield and bouncing off, while you stay totally safe and protected inside.

I like to visualize the shield as a large invisible bubble surrounding me. This means I'm protected in every direction.

The circle of protection works well on its own, but it can be made even more powerful with the help of your crystal. Touch or rub your crystal while you're inside the circle of protection, and imagine it giving you unlimited strength and confidence. You'll feel like laughing at any stress that comes your way and will be able to stand up for yourself easily and effectively.

How to Protect Loved Ones

You can also send protection to the special people in your life when you're apart. You might like to send protection to your partner at work, your children at school, close friends, and anyone else who you feel would benefit from added protection.

This is a simple ritual that you can do anywhere, at any time, whether sitting, standing, lying down, or walking.

1. Fondle your crystal and mentally tell it what you're planning to do. Hold the crystal in your hands throughout the ritual.

2. Take several slow, deep breaths to help you relax and get into the right frame of mind for the ritual.

3. Close your eyes for about thirty seconds and visualize the person you're sending protection to. If you're sitting at your desk at work or are out walking, keep your eyes open while visualizing the person. Hold the image of the person in your mind for as long as you can.

4. Take three slow, deep breaths. Inhale as much oxygen as you can, hold your breath for a few seconds, and exhale slowly. With each inhalation, visualize that you're filling yourself to overflowing with divine energy.

5. Mentally send all this energy and protection to the person you're thinking about. Visualize them surrounded by a protective shield that was created by your breath.

6. Send thoughts of love to the person you've just protected.

7. Take three or four deep breaths to recharge yourself. If your eyes are still closed, this is the time to open them again.

8. Thank the Universal Life Force for enabling you to psychically protect your loved ones. Rub your crystal and thank it for helping you.

9. When you feel ready, carry on with your day.

This ritual is a simple one that can be performed in just a few minutes. Despite its simplicity, it's extremely powerful. On several occasions, people have told me that they felt my presence or suddenly thought of me at the exact moment I was sending them protection. I'm sure you'll hear similar stories from your loved ones when you start performing this ritual.

How to Ward Off a Psychic Attack

A psychic attack occurs when one person maliciously or unintentionally attempts to harm another person by sending them negative energy. It can be done intentionally if the person focuses and sends negative energy to the chosen victim. It can also occur unintentionally when someone has negative thoughts about someone else.

A prolonged psychic attack can cause stress, worry, illness, and even death. Fortunately, an attack of this sort is extremely rare, but minor attacks do occur regularly. Jealousy, resentment, and struggles for power are common reasons for a psychic attack. Anyone who appears to be slightly different can become a target for other people. Verbal abuse is another form of attack.

If you learn, or even suspect, that you're being psychically attacked, there are several things you can do to protect yourself:

- Carry your crystal with you at all times.

- Ground yourself. Spend time outdoors and touch the earth. Visit a park or beautiful garden.

- Exercise to strengthen your aura. A good walk is all that's required, but do something more vigorous if you're able to. As well as strengthening your aura, all exercise releases endorphins, which provide additional protection.

- Send thoughts of love to everyone you know. It makes no difference if they're friends or foes.

- Take salt baths. Prepare a relaxing bath incorporating two parts baking soda to one part salt when you're experiencing a psychic attack.

- Keep yourself protected inside a circle of protection.

- Eat healthy foods to keep your strength up. Avoid sugary foods and drinks. Drink plenty of water.

- Call on a higher power for help.

- Laugh as much as you can. Spend time with friends who make you laugh, and watch comedies and stand-up comedians.

- Nurture yourself in some way. Do something purely for the fun of it.

Keep your crystal with you while doing these things. Remember to thank it for all the help it's giving you.

15: SPIRITUAL GUIDANCE

Your crystal can help you enter a deeply relaxed meditative state in which you can ask for guidance and help and receive answers from the Divine. You don't need a religious background to do this. In fact, it makes no difference if you're religious or not.

The simplest way to use your crystal to communicate with the Divine is to hold it in your hands while praying. I find it useful to write down everything I need help with before making the prayer. This ensures that I don't accidentally forget something while I'm praying.

It's a good idea to make a ritual of your prayer. You can do this by using the same location whenever possible, surrounding yourself with sacred objects, and perhaps lighting a candle or two.

Speak to the Divine as if you were talking to a close friend. Speak in your normal manner. You don't need to use formal or old-fashioned words. In fact, any words you use will be the right ones, as they'll be unique to you.

You can pray silently or out loud. Obviously you'll pray silently if you're praying while waiting in line at the supermarket. In the privacy of your own home, you can pray in any way that feels right for you.

Some people worry about what to say when they're praying. You don't need to say anything specific. All you need do is to open your heart and mind to the Divine.

There is no special format for a prayer. If you know a prayer of any sort, such as the Lord's Prayer, you might start with that and then tell the Divine about your problems and desires. You shouldn't feel guilty about praying for something for yourself. You are just as worthy as anyone else. Pray for others, of course, but also pray for yourself.

Archangel Crystal Ritual

This is a ritual to prepare your crystal for its new role in helping you to make instant communication with the Divine.

Required: a small table to act as an altar, five or more white candles, a container of water, and a small container of salt.

Before starting the ritual, have a leisurely bath or shower and change into fresh, loose-fitting clothes.

1. Place your altar in the center of your work space, and place your crystal, container of water, small container of salt, and a candle on it.

2. Mark out a circle that you'll work within. You can do this with a cord, candles, or small objects that are sacred to you. I use a circular rug to indicate my prayer space, and for the purposes of this ritual, use four candles to indicate the four cardinal directions.

3. Step inside your circle and light the candle on your altar. (If you're using candles to indicate the four directions, light them first, starting with the candle at the east, followed by the candles in the south, west,

and north.) Pick up your crystal, and hold it at chest height in the palm of your right hand, which should rest on your left hand. Close your eyes and visualize or imagine that you're surrounded and protected by the four great archangels: Raphael, Michael, Gabriel, and Uriel.

4. Turn to face the east and talk to Raphael, telling him that you wish to consecrate your crystal so that you can contact the Divine. You might say something along the lines of "Archangel Raphael, thank you for being with me today. I am very grateful to you for your help and protection. I ask you to bless this crystal, so I may use it to contact the Divine. Thank you." Pause until you receive a response. The responses you'll receive from the archangels can come in different ways. You might hear something, but it's more likely that you'll have a sense of knowing that each archangel has given assent to your request.

5. Speak to all the archangels in the same way. After Raphael in the east, turn ninety degrees to Michael in the south, followed by Gabriel in the west, and Uriel in the north.

6. After you've spoken to the four archangels, hold the crystal against your heart chakra. When you feel ready, hold the crystal in your right palm and talk to it. "I have the blessing of the four mighty archangels

to use you to contact the Divine. I'm now going to consecrate you with the elements of fire, air, water, and earth."

7. Pass the crystal through the flame of the candle, while saying, "I now consecrate you with the element of fire." Pass the crystal through the smoke produced by the candle while saying, "I now consecrate you with the element of air." Place the crystal on your altar. Dip your fingers into the container of water and sprinkle some water onto your crystal while saying, "I now consecrate you with the element of water." Pick up some grains of salt and sprinkle them onto the crystal while saying, "I now consecrate you with the element of earth."

8. Pick up the crystal again and hold it in the palm of your right hand, which should be resting on your left palm. Thank it for helping you communicate with the Divine. Say, "Thank you for agreeing to help me. I will look after you to the best of my ability." Turn in a slow circle, showing your crystal to each of the archangels while thanking them for their help and support.

9. Place your crystal on your altar in front of the candle. (If you used candles to indicate the four directions, snuff them out first.) Snuff out the candle on the altar and close the circle. Do this by removing the objects

that indicate the four directions. Start with the east, followed by south, west, and north. Remove any other items that you may have used to indicate the circle. Finally, remove the objects on the altar and place the altar back where it came from.

Your crystal is now ready for use. Hold it whenever you need to communicate with the Divine, and touch it whenever you need courage or confidence.

16: YOUR CRYSTAL AND SELF-IMPROVEMENT

Self-improvement is the act of improving ourselves. People have been interested in improving their quality of life since at least the time of the ancient Greeks. We can focus on our habits, thoughts, and actions to improve any aspect of our lives, including education, happiness, health, relationships, spirituality, money, and career. Your crystal can help you do this.

A friend of mine is using her crystal to learn a foreign language before making her first visit to France. When I congratulated her on how disciplined she was, she laughingly told me that her crystal kept her on track. I knew she'd programmed it to help her learn the language, and she was happy to tell me how she was getting on. She keeps the crystal on her dining room table, and whenever she sees it, it motivates her to start studying.

Self-Esteem

You have good self-esteem when you feel good about yourself. You need good self-esteem to be successful in life. When you love and respect yourself, others will reflect this back to you. Likewise, before you can love others, you must love yourself. You'll have good self-esteem when you know that the only thing that matters is what you think about yourself. What other people think about you is not important.

Everyone is born with good self-esteem. Unfortunately, as children grow up they're constantly exposed to negativity, sometimes even from the people who love them the most, and many people emerge as adults who feel unable to love and respect themselves.

Confidence

Most people express a desire for more confidence whenever the subject of self-improvement comes up. Confidence is a fascinating topic, as everyone is confident in some areas of their life, but lacks confidence in others. You may, for instance, feel totally confident when dealing with coworkers, but find it hard to interact with people at social functions. I used to know an auctioneer who could stand up and entertain a crowd of strangers while selling cars, but avoided social functions because he felt inadequate.

We're all different, but fortunately we can all use our crystal whenever we feel the need for more confidence.

Try this:

1. Think about your need for confidence and self-esteem, and write down a list of all the areas you need help with.

2. Turn each of these into a positive affirmation written in the present tense, as if you already possess all the confidence you need. You might, for instance, write "I find it hard to stand up for myself and

always end up doing what the other person wants."
You could turn that into a positive affirmation along
the lines of "I am assertive and speak my mind in a
kind and caring manner. I stand up for myself." Do
this for everything you wrote down.

3. In addition to this, write down some general affirmations relating to confidence, such as "I have
good self-esteem; I am loved and respected; I respect
others and am worthy of their respect in return; I
am secure and supremely confident in every type of
situation; I am a positive, happy person; I believe in
myself; I release negative thoughts and feelings; and
I deserve all the good things that the world has
to offer."

4. Cleanse your crystal and dedicate it to your need for
confidence.

5. Hold your crystal in your cupped hands and blow
your energy onto it.

6. Close your hands over your crystal, and say—ideally
out loud, but silently if necessary—all the affirmations you've created. Put passion and power into
each one, and allow a few seconds of silence between
them. As you do this, visualize the energy and power
of your words imprinting themselves inside
your crystal.

7. Once you've done this, while still holding the crystal, close your eyes and think about a typical day. If you're doing this exercise at the start of your day, think about the day ahead. At other times, think about a typical day for you. It's a normal day in every way, except for one difference. In the day you're visualizing, you have all the confidence and self-esteem that you need to handle anything that comes your way. Hold this scenario in your mind for as long as you can. See yourself dealing with situations that would have been difficult in the past, but handling them with ease and confidence.

8. Squeeze your crystal between your hands and think about how wonderful your life is going to be in the future now that you have the confidence and self-esteem you need.

9. Open your eyes and carry on with your day. Keep your crystal with you all the time. Hold it, fondle it, or touch it whenever you feel the need for a boost in confidence. Do this before going into any situations that you think might be difficult, but also do it at odd moments during the day.

Once you've written down your affirmations, this exercise can be done in just a few minutes. Do it at least once a day until you become the person you want to be. You can add new affirmations or remove affirmations that you no longer need whenever you wish.

It's important, when you do this, that you face up to situations that require confidence and self-esteem. It's all very well to visualize, but at some stage you need to prove to yourself that you can do and accomplish everything you picture in your mind.

You can use the same process to program your crystal for all forms of self-improvement. You might do it before taking on a new role at work, for instance, or to gain motivation to achieve a particular task.

17: KEEPING IN TOUCH WITH DISTANT FRIENDS

Friendships are among the greatest blessings in life, and it's always sad when a good friend moves away. Fortunately, you can use your crystal to keep in touch with friends, no matter where in the world they happen to be.

You can give a friend who is far away from you a crystal that has been worn on your body for two or three weeks and charged with love and friendship. When this person holds the crystal, they will feel your energy and feelings. Holding the crystal will provide happiness as well as comfort, depending on the situation.

The benefits of this can be increased many times if you and your friend exchange suitably charged crystals. If you wish, you can create a ritual involving the exchanging of crystals.

1. You and your friend should wear the crystals next to the body for at least two weeks before the ritual begins.

2. Start the ritual by having a conversation about your friendship and how much you'll miss each other. While doing this, you should each remove your crystal and place it in your friend's palm. You should each hold your hands so they're touching each other. Remain in this position for at least sixty seconds to enable the crystals to be fully charged and energized.

3. Place your crystal around your friend's neck. Have your friend place their crystal around your neck.

4. Complete the ritual by talking again about your friendship, and how it is so important to you both that you promise to do everything you can to keep the friendship alive.

Any time you happen to see or feel the crystal in the future, you need to remember your promise and send friendship and love to your friend. Every time we think of someone, we're establishing a psychic bond. You already have a strong psychic connection to your friend, but each time you think of them the connection will grow stronger, and the crystal will help make it happen. Energy always follows thought.

When thinking of someone special who is far away, it's worth remembering that they are still with you mentally, emotionally, and spiritually. The only part that's missing is their physical body. You can still communicate with your friend in many ways, such as by Skype, phone, email, or text message. Communicate regularly with your friend to keep the bond alive. Each time you do this, hold your crystal in your left hand and fondle or stroke it every now and again. If you and your friend do this each time you communicate, you'll gradually build up a strong psychic, emotional, and mental connection and will ultimately be able to start communicating telepathically with each other.

Crystal Telepathy

Telepathy is the art of mind-to-mind communication. It often occurs spontaneously in a time of crisis. There are many recorded instances of people suddenly knowing that something bad has happened to someone they care about. Telepathy can occur in the form of a dream, a picture in the mind, or as a thought or feeling.

Here's an experiment you and your friend can try. Conduct it in a light-hearted, carefree manner, as you're more likely to be successful that way. Don't expect instant results and don't stop communicating in other ways.

1. Agree on a time when you and your friend can experiment for ten minutes. You will need to agree on which person will transmit thoughts for the first five minutes, while the other person receives thoughts. After five minutes, the roles change, and the initial sender becomes the receiver, and vice versa.

2. Two or three minutes before the start of the experiment, sit down with your crystal in your hand, take several slow, deep breaths, and relax.

3. When the experiment starts, the person who is doing the sending needs to think of the receiver and send them any thoughts or messages they wish. After doing this for five minutes, the roles change and the receiver becomes the sender and transmits thoughts and messages for five minutes. Each person needs to

write down any thoughts they pick up while receiving. You might need to put your crystal down while doing this. If so, place it somewhere you can see it while you're writing.

4. The final stage is to contact each other and evaluate the results. You may experience good results on your first attempt. Don't worry if you don't, as your results will improve with practice.

Photographic Communication

This is an interesting experiment you can try with good friends who may or may not live far from you. You and your friend will each have to collect at least five photographs of people in your respective families. Each photograph can contain only one person in it, and all the people in the photographs should be known to the friend.

Arrange a time for the experiment. Before starting, you and your friend should lay the photographs out in a row. One of you is selected to be the transmitter. This person places their crystal on top of one of the photographs in front of them When the experiment starts, this person thinks about the person in the photograph for two minutes. Then the transmitter picks up the crystal and places it down again, either on a different photograph, or the same one as before. Again, they think about the person in the photograph that the crystal is resting on. This is done a third time. While this is happening, the receiver tries to pick up thoughts that identify the person the transmitter is think-ing about.

After six minutes is up, the roles change and the transmitter becomes the receiver, and vice versa. The new transmitter places a crystal on a photograph and thinks about that person for two minutes. Once they have done this three times, the two people contact each other and see how well they did.

With practice, the success rate will increase. This is a sign to increase the number of photographs to ten.

18: YOUR CRYSTAL AND RELATIONSHIPS

Successful relationships manage to survive no matter how many problems they experience. They have a number of things in common. In addition to love, they have trust, honesty, forgiveness, compromise, loyalty, communication, and respect. These qualities enable good relationships to strengthen and grow over time. Sadly, many relationships lack these qualities, which is why approximately half of all marriages fail. This is tragic when you think that all of these couples must have entered the marriage thinking it would last forever.

People in successful relationships do many things, consciously or unconsciously, that support and sustain their relationships. They work on them. When problems arise, they address them right away. They communicate with each other. They spend quality time together, but also allow each other space for individual interests. They accept the other person as they are, and don't try to change them. At times, they agree to disagree. They respect and support their partner, and don't take them for granted. They do everything they can to sustain the romance in their relationship.

Most of these apply to friendships and other non-romantic relationships as well.

You can use your crystal to enhance your existing relationships, and to encourage new relationships.

How to Enhance an Existing Relationship

You'll find this ritual useful for enhancing an existing relationship. All you need is about thirty minutes of time and a partner who is interested in crystals, or is at least willing to suspend disbelief for thirty minutes. Find a comfortable place where you're unlikely to be disturbed. Start by showing your partner your crystal, and tell them that you intend to carry it with you to make your relationship even better than it currently is. Ask your partner if they are willing to take part in a short ritual with the crystal. If your partner agrees, you can continue.

1. Tell your partner that you're going to hold the crystal for about ten minutes to imbue it with your energy. Place the crystal in your palm and close your fingers over it. Hold hands with your partner using your other hand.

2. Enjoy a pleasant chat with your partner for about ten minutes. Once the time is up, give them the crystal to hold, and continue the conversation for at least another ten minutes.

3. The final stage is for you both to hold the crystal together for about ten minutes. Place the crystal in the palm of your hand and ask your partner to place their palm over yours, enclosing the crystal between the two palms. Allow your fingers to close over the side of your partner's hand. Again, continue conversing for about ten minutes.

4. Finish the ritual by saying something along the lines of "I dedicate this crystal to the two of us. May it bring joy and love into every part of our relationship."

5. Keep the crystal with you, and hold or fondle it whenever you can. Each time you do this, you'll think of your partner, and they may pick up your thoughts telepathically.

If your partner shows interest in what you're doing, you could give them a crystal to carry. After cleansing and dedicating it, all you need do is go through the above ritual again with the new crystal. Once you've done that, place the two crystals side by side in direct sunlight or moonlight, and then both of you can enjoy the benefits of carrying a loving crystal everywhere you go.

Resolving Problems in Relationships

All relationships, romantic or otherwise, have their ups and downs, and these difficulties need to be resolved to prevent the situation from becoming worse than it already is. Fortunately, your crystal can help you do this.

In addition to your crystal, you'll need a photograph of the two of you enjoying a happy moment together. A wedding photograph is a good example. If you don't have a suitable photograph, write your name and your partner's name on a sheet of paper and use that instead.

1. Sit down comfortably with the photograph in one hand and your crystal in the other. Gaze at the photograph and recall everything you can about what was going on when it was taken. Recapture the feelings and emotions you felt at the time. If you wrote the names on a sheet of paper, gaze at them and think about a time when you and your partner were supremely happy.

2. While gazing at the photograph (or sheet of paper) affirm this to yourself several times: "(Name of partner) and I love each other unconditionally. Our relationship is strong and powerful, and is becoming stronger and more powerful every day. I love him (her), and he (she) loves me."

3. Squeeze the crystal in your hand and repeat the affirmation again.

4. Carry on with your day.

You should repeat this ritual every day until the relationship is back to normal. Whenever you have a spare moment, touch the crystal and think of the love you and your partner share. If you and your partner quarrel, touch your crystal and silently repeat the affirmation.

How to Attract Friends

Ralph Waldo Emerson, the American poet and philosopher, wrote that "the only way to have a friend is to be one." I once told this to an introverted man I knew who complained that he had no friends. He retorted that what Emerson wrote was all very well, but the first step was to meet people, and he couldn't do that. Like everyone else, he met many people during his everyday life, but was unable to establish a connection with any of them.

I gave him a series of visualizations in which he saw himself interacting successfully with others. It took time, but eventually he developed some social skills and ultimately made friends.

If you're finding it hard to make friends, relax somewhere with your crystal and visualize yourself having a good time with people who have similar interests as you. In your mind's eye, see yourself talking, sharing laughter, and spending quality time together. Hold your crystal tightly and ask it to help you find good friends.

Carry the crystal around with you, and repeat this exercise regularly until you make friends. In addition to this, focus on being a friend. Once you've taken the first step a few times, you'll enjoy doing this and it will speed up the process of making friends.

19: ATTRACTING LOVE

Crystals and gemstones have been used as amulets to attract love for thousands of years. In *Lithica*, a fourth-century epic poem about crystals, the anonymous author wrote that gemstones were much better at attracting love than herbs, because herbs lose their power while gemstones retain their effectiveness forever (Gifford 1963, 119).

Many people are sad and lonely because they lack love in their lives. This can be caused by many things. Sometimes someone may have suffered badly in a relationship and decided not to allow anyone to get close to them ever again. Another person may be so timid and introverted that they find it impossible to establish a loving relationship. These people are leading half-lives, as they're depriving themselves of the pleasures, joys, and happiness that a good, stable, loving relationship provides.

If this is a factor in your life, and you want to attract love, you should perform this ritual to help create the right environment for love to occur. All you need is your crystal and a sheet of pink paper or cardboard about 8 ½ by 11 inches.

1. Stand the pink card on a table or shelf. Place a chair about six feet away from it. When you're sitting on the chair you should be able to look at the pink card without raising or lowering your head or eyes.

2. Sit down on the chair with your crystal in your left hand (right hand if you're left-handed).

3. Take several slow, deep breaths while staring at the pink cardboard.

4. Close your eyes and visualize the pink energy growing until you're completely surrounded by pink energy.

5. Take several slow, deep breaths and visualize this calming, loving energy spreading into every cell of your body.

6. Affirm to yourself: "I am love. I attract nothing but good relationships into my life."

7. Hold your crystal tightly and continue visualizing yourself inside a cloud of loving, pink energy for as long as you can.

8. When the visualization fades, say thank you to the universe and open your eyes.

How to Attract the Right Person into Your Life

The need to love and be loved is one of the most fundamental needs that humans have. If you're on your own and are seeking a loving relationship, you can use your crystal to attract the right person into your life.

The first step is to be sure that you're ready for a new relationship. If you've had nothing but disappointment in the past, you might be worried about undergoing the same stress and pain again. Consequently, you should choose your new partner carefully.

1. Sit down comfortably with your crystal in your hand. Close your eyes and take several slow, deep breaths to relax your body. Think about the qualities you want any new partner to possess. Some of these are likely to be non-negotiable qualities, while others might be desirable, but not essential.

2. Once you've thought about the desirable qualities, think about the qualities that you don't want in your prospective partner. Are you prepared to compromise on any of these?

3. The next stage is to think about yourself. You've thought about the partner you desire, but what are you prepared to do to make and keep him or her happy?

4. Visualize yourself in the company of your ideal partner. Picture them exhibiting all the qualities you desire. See yourself happy, laughing, and thoroughly enjoying life. Squeeze your crystal and hold on to the image for as long as you can.

5. When the image starts to fade, tell yourself that you're starting to attract the right person, one with all the qualities that you desire. Ideally, say this out loud with as much conviction as you can. If you're unable to speak openly for any reason, say it silently with a smile on your face.

6. Open your eyes, take a few deep breaths, stretch, and get up.

Be patient, stay positive, and repeat this exercise every day until you've attracted a good loving relationship into your life.

20: HELPING CHILDREN WITH YOUR CRYSTAL

Children relate extremely well to crystals. They help them balance their spiritual, emotional, and physical natures. Tumbled stones are usually the best form of crystal to give to a child, as they are smooth and have appealing colors.

Once you give a stone or crystal to a child, you're likely to be surprised at the amount of information they will glean from it. Of course, children vary in how they respond to the subtle energies of a crystal. Some will immediately welcome the crystal into their lives, while others will be more cautious.

A friend of mine gave crystals to her son and daughter as an experiment. She worked regularly with crystals, and thought that because of this, her children would be delighted to have a crystal of their own. The daughter was excited and started communicating with her crystal right away. Her twelve-year-old son immediately placed his on top of his wardrobe. A few days later, he put it into a small box and placed it under his bed. She thought he didn't like the crystal, until a few weeks later when he told her that it protected him while he was asleep.

If you're a parent, you can program your child's crystals to provide protection, deal with emotions, encourage creativity, boost confidence, remove blockages, calm and ground them, or do anything else to help.

Once you've done this, you can encourage the child to wear or carry it in a small pouch. Alternatively, you might sew it into a pillow, place it under a mattress, or place it somewhere close to the child's bed.

Crystals can help children fall asleep. If a child is finding it hard to sleep for any reason, give them a crystal to hold, and ask them to send happy thoughts to the crystal. Ideally, the child should be lying down in bed with their eyes closed. However, although it's intended to send children to sleep, this can be done at any time. A lady I know used it to calm her children down whenever they became overactive. She told me that her children usually fell asleep when doing this exercise at night, but during the day it helped them relax and quiet down. Obviously, this exercise should be performed only with children who are old enough to not place crystals in their mouths.

Placing a crystal under a child's pillow can be helpful if they suffer from nightmares or frequent wakefulness.

You'll find the child will be keen to help you cleanse gemstones. It's a good idea to use the four elements for this. Here is a version of this that doesn't use a candle to signify fire and air. Ideally, this should be performed on a sunny, breezy day.

Four Elements Cleansing

Required: a bowl of water and a small container of salt

1. Give the stone to the child and ask them to hold it with cupped hands (the back of the right hand resting on the palm of the left hand). Go outside and face east. Ask the child to hold the stone in the breeze for about two minutes. After a couple of minutes, you both can say, "I cleanse this stone with the power and energy of air."

2. You and the child should turn to face south and place the gemstone in the full light of the sun. Wait two or three minutes, and then both say, "I cleanse this stone with the power and energy of fire."

3. You should both turn to the west. Place the gemstone in the bowl of water and ask the child to wash it. Once this has been done, the child can dry it with a towel, before holding it in their cupped hands. Both of you can say, "I cleanse this stone with the power and energy of water." (If you live close to a stream or river, you might choose to use that instead of a bowl of water.)

4. Turn to face north. If you have a reasonable amount of salt, you can bury the gemstone in it for a few minutes. Alternatively, you can hold the stone and ask the child to sprinkle grains of salt onto it.

(A third method is to bury the stone in the earth for a few days. In my experience, most children will prefer a faster method.) You both should say, "I cleanse this stone with the power and energy of earth."

5. The final stage is to fill the gemstone with positive energy. Ask the child to hold the stone in their cupped hands. Ask the child to close their eyes, and ask them to think of the happiest thing they can think of, and to keep thinking of it for as long as they can. When the thought fades, the child opens their eyes and the stone is ready for use. In practice, I like to have the child fill the crystal with positive energy. If the child is too young, or doesn't want to do it, you can do it yourself. Another method is to leave the stone in the rays of the sun for a few hours.

21: YOUR CRYSTAL AND HAPPINESS

Happiness is a difficult word to define, as it's very subjective. What makes me happy might do nothing at all for you, and vice versa. Yet we both, like everybody else, want to be happy. In psychology, happiness is defined as a state of well-being that includes contentment, positive emotions, and satisfaction with life.

Obviously, no one can be happy all the time. Everyone has ups and downs in their life. However, naturally happy people overcome the negative times more quickly than other people, and regain their natural positivity.

Happiness is considered so important that it appears in the United States Declaration of Independence as an unalienable right: "Life, liberty and the pursuit of happiness." This encourages people to pursue happiness in any way they wish, provided it doesn't break the law or violate the rights of others.

More than thirty years ago, Tai L'au, a feng shui master, gave me some valuable advice. He said, "If you want to be happy, be happy." This is particularly good advice since happiness comes from within. A large pay raise, for instance, will make you happy for a short while, but before long you'll return to the state of happiness you were in before you received the increase in pay. I've seen happy people in slums and have met deeply unhappy people living in mansions.

Once your basic needs are met, additional money is only ever a temporary source of happiness.

A sense of gratitude improves relationships as well as providing feelings of joy and happiness. It can be a useful (not to mention happiness producing) exercise to write down five or six things you're grateful for. If you do this every week, you'll be amazed at how much you should be thankful for, and this will make a profound difference to your happiness levels.

You should make an effort to do something you enjoy every day. I know you're busy, but you must make time for something that makes you happy. I love walking and derive great pleasure from it. Consequently, no matter what sort of day I've had, I immediately brighten up when I make time for a walk.

Your crystal can also help you become happier.

1. Start by thinking of something that makes you happy. It doesn't matter what it is, as long as you can clearly visualize it.

2. Sit down in a comfortable chair. Hold your crystal in your cupped hands. Think about what's going on in your life, and ask yourself what you can do to become happier than you currently are.

3. Close your eyes and gently squeeze your crystal. Take a few slow, deep breaths to help you relax, and then think about whatever it is that makes you happy.

As clearly as you possibly can, relive a happy experience in your mind. See yourself, happily involved in the experience.

4. Once you've relived the experience for as long as you can, let it go and become aware of your physical body. Check your heart and throat chakras, and scan your body to see how relaxed you are. Squeeze your crystal and ask yourself if you're feeling happy. If you are, enjoy the feeling for as long as possible. When you feel ready, open your eyes and carry on with your day. If you're not feeling a sense of happiness, open your eyes, stand up, and stretch. Walk around for a minute or two, then repeat the experiment with a different happy memory. You can do this immediately, or if your time is limited, go through the steps again on the following day.

5. Once you experience joy and happiness after doing this exercise, your crystal will be automatically dedicated to enhancing the amount of happiness you experience in life. Whenever you need a boost of happiness, all you need do is touch or hold your crystal and you'll immediately notice a sense of positivity and happiness.

You're not restricted to one happy memory. You can use as many as you wish while doing this exercise. It's hard to remain unhappy when you're reliving several happy memories, one after the other.

22: CREATING A SACRED SPACE

Joseph Campbell, the American mythologist and writer, described sacred space as a place where wonder can be revealed. A sacred space is an area in or around your home that you can use for rituals, meditation, reflection, prayer, spirituality, mindfulness, and contacting the Divine. It makes no difference how large or small it is.

Before starting to create a sacred space, you need to decide what you'll be using the space for and how often you'll be using it. A sacred space that is used once a week can be set up each time you use it, but you'll probably want a more permanent display if you're going to be using it every day.

You may also want to discuss your plans with other members of the household. Will everyone be able to use the sacred space, or will it be reserved solely for you? If you have children, will you let them use it too? If you're going to use it privately, will you tell other members of the household about your sacred space? You may need to keep it secret if you're living with people who don't understand your spiritual beliefs.

Your sacred space needs to be somewhere quiet where you won't be interrupted by others while you're using it. You might be fortunate and have a spare room that could be used. If you can't find a small amount of space anywhere, you might want to keep everything you require for your sacred space in a box, and set up your sacred space wherever you find room, such as on a table or bed. Another alternative is to use a rug. It can be kept rolled up when you're not using it, and laid on the floor when you use it to mark out your sacred space. A prayer rug or a meditation cushion are also possibilities. My first sacred space was outdoors. I live in a temperate climate and could use it almost all year.

You can place anything you wish inside your sacred space. You might have an altar. If so, you can place candles, your crystal, and any other items that you find attractive on it. There is no limit to what you can place in your sacred space—books, ornamental statues, divination tools, incense, paintings, musical bowls, shells, stones, flowers, plants, fruits, and anything else that feels sacred to you. You might also like to have a source of music inside your sacred space.

Once your sacred space has been set up, you need to clear it of any negative energies. If you have a permanent sacred space, you might use a smudge stick to clear the space. Musical bowls, prayers, chants, and sacred songs can also be used to initiate a sacred space. You can clear temporary sacred spaces by walking around the area with your crystal in your cupped hands. Alternatively, you can stand in the center of your sacred space and clap your hands while turning in a circle. You can light candles with the intention of illuminating your sacred space with all that is good.

You can do anything you wish inside your sacred space. You'll find that the more you use it, the more sacred the space will become, and the more it will play an important role in your life.

I use my sacred space for several purposes. I often sit there when I'm trying to make sense of life. I do my personal spiritual work there. I read spiritual books inside my sacred space. I perform divinations for family members. I perform rituals inside my sacred space. Sometimes I meditate there, using a crystal as the focus. I've found that whenever I feel anxious or stressed, a minute or two in my sacred space, while holding my crystal, rejuvenates me.

Here's a brief blessing ritual that I frequently perform in my sacred space.

Required: a crystal, three white candles, and a jug of water. (The water plays no part in the ritual, but is placed beside the altar to put out the candles in an emergency. I have never needed to use it, but always have water handy in case of an accident.) If you don't have an altar or table, you'll need a stable surface to place the candles on.

1. Place one candle in the center of the altar. Place the second candle to the left of the first one, and the third candle to the right of the first candle. Place your crystal on the altar in front of the central candle.

2. Stand, sit, or kneel in front of the altar and speak to the Universal Life Force. You might say, "I am here today to thank you for all the blessings you have given me. You gave me the gift of life, and all the delights and pleasures of this world. I am very grateful." Pick up the crystal and stroke or fondle it for several seconds before replacing it on your altar.

3. Light the center candle. Step back and gaze at the candle flame. Silently or out loud, express your gratitude to the Universal Life Force for the life you're living. Think or talk about special moments in your life. These could be happy, sad, tragic, moving, life-changing, or loving. If you find it hard to think of anything specific, choose a single episode from each decade of your life and talk about that. Once you've finished speaking, pick up your crystal and stroke or fondle it for several seconds. Then replace it on your altar. Close your eyes and say thank you.

4. When you feel ready, open your eyes and light the candle on your left. Step back and gaze at the flame of this candle. Think about your family, and visualize yourself at the front of the long line of people who have come before you. Thank them for being part of your history and for playing a major role in your makeup. Think about other family members—siblings, uncles, aunts, cousins, and any other members of your wider family. Thank them all for their love and support. Thank the Universal Life Force for enabling you to play a vital role in this family. When you've finished thinking about your family, pick up the crystal and stroke or fondle it for several seconds. Place it back on your altar. Close your eyes and say thank you.

5. When you feel ready, open your eyes and light the candle on your right. Step back and gaze into the flame of this candle. Think about all the other people you care about in this lifetime. Think about childhood friends, work colleagues, friends you see frequently, and others you see rarely. Think about your teachers, coaches, mentors, and anyone else who has given you encouragement and support. Think about the special people in your life. Thank the Universal Life Force for enabling you to meet and love all of these people. Pick up your crystal and stroke it for several seconds. Continue fondling it until the end of the ritual. Close your eyes and say thank you.

6. Open your eyes. Gaze at the flames on the three candles and thank the Universal Life Force for all it has done for you and for all that it will continue to do for you in this lifetime.

7. Continue looking at the candles for as long as you wish. When you're ready, say, "I am truly blessed. Thank you."

Snuff the candles, starting with the one on the right, then the one on the left, and finally the one in the middle.

23: YOUR CRYSTAL AND SPIRITUAL GROWTH

Crystals have always been associated with spirituality. As crystals can convert and harmonize energy into a spiritual form, they can help you make your prayers more effective. Your crystal will help you enter the desired meditative state to communicate with Spirit, no matter what name you use (such as God, Universal Life Force, the Ultimate, Jehovah, Elohim, Allah, or Holy Spirit). When you do this, you're channeling.

Channeling is the art of communicating with the spirit world. It has been practiced for thousands of years by the Assyrians, Babylonians, Chinese, Egyptians, Japanese, Indians, Romans, and Tibetans. It has also played an important role in Christianity and Judaism.

Channeling can be performed through many means, including meditation, prayer, hypnosis, dancing, and chanting. Here is a useful method of channeling that you can perform with your crystal:

1. One day before performing the ritual, write a letter to God (using whichever name you prefer. For the sake of convenience, I'll use Universal Life Force). Tell the Universal Life Force something about your life. Explain as clearly as you can why you're writing the letter. This is necessary, even if your aim is purely

to thank the Universal Life Force for enabling you to enjoy a life of happiness and fulfillment. Finish by thanking the Universal Life Force for attending to your request. Don't sign the letter yet. During the next twenty-four hours, think of additions you can make to the letter. There may also be sections you'd like to delete and areas that you'd like to expand. Make any changes you wish to your letter, and this time when you've finished, sign it.

2. Sit down comfortably in a warm room, with your feet flat on the ground and your hands in your lap. Your letter should be resting on a nearby table or on the floor beside you. The back of your left hand should be resting on the palm of your right hand, and your crystal should be lying on your left palm.

3. Close your eyes and take several slow, deep breaths. On each exhalation, say to yourself, "Relax, relax, relax" or "I'm calm and relaxed." Feel your muscles relaxing with each exhalation.

4. Once you're fully relaxed, think of your purpose for holding the ritual. Open your eyes and pick up your letter. Open it and read it out loud. Put the letter away, close your eyes, and allow yourself to relax again.

5. When you feel completely relaxed, imagine the room you're in filling up with a cloud-like white light. Visualize it as clearly as you can.

6. When the room is completely full of white light, you'll feel a wave of ineffable peace pass over you, and the energy of the room will change. You'll have a sense of knowing that you're in the presence of the Universal Life Force. Rub your crystal gently and say hello. Wait quietly for a response. You probably won't be able to tell if the Universal Life Force is talking directly to you or if the words are appearing in your mind. Either way, once you've established communication, you'll be able to converse easily and fluently. Much to your surprise, you'll feel calm and relaxed and will have no difficulty replying to the Universal Life Force's questions and asking for whatever it is you want.

7. You'll feel you can talk for as long as you wish, as the Universal Life Force will be in no hurry to end the conversation. When the conversation comes to an end, thank the Universal Life Force for everything it is doing for you, and say goodbye.

8. Remain in your chair, gently caress your crystal, and take several slow, deep breaths while the white light dissipates. Enjoy the peace and calmness you feel throughout your entire body.

9. Get up and carry on with your day. Keep the letter and your crystal with you. At least once a day, read your letter to the Universal Life Force. Continue doing this until your request is granted.

It's a good idea to write down everything you can recall about your conversation with the Universal Life Force, as you're likely to have covered much more than you included in your letter.

Obviously this is not a ritual you should do every day. It is intended to be used whenever you have a problem or situation that is proving hard to resolve.

Here's a shorter ritual of thanks that you can do whenever you wish.

Before you start, think of two or three things you'd like to thank the Universal Life Force for. These can be major or minor. You might give thanks for the gift of life and, at the same time, give thanks because someone you like smiled at you.

1. Sit down comfortably with your crystal resting on your cupped palms.

2. Close your eyes and take several deep breaths, silently saying "Relax, relax, relax" as you exhale.

3. When you feel totally relaxed, rub your crystal and ask the Universal Life Force to join you. Continue taking slow, deep breaths and rubbing your crystal as you wait for a sign that the Universal Life Force is with you. This is likely to come as a sense of knowing that the Universal Life Force has arrived. It could also come as a small voice inside your head. (This is called clairaudience.)

4. Once you're sure that the Universal Life Force is present, thank him/her for coming, and then express your thanks for all the blessings you have in your life, including the two items you thought of earlier. Tell the Universal Life Force that you're doing the best you can and are grateful to him/her for helping and loving you. Offer your love in return.

5. Say goodbye to the Universal Life Force. Sit quietly for a minute or two, thinking about your meeting. When you're ready, open your eyes and continue with your day. You'll feel blessed, happy, and full of energy after this ritual.

Keep your crystal with you. Every time you touch it, you'll think of the Universal Life Force and everything he/she is doing for you.

24: PRAYING WITH A CRYSTAL

People have prayed throughout history. Even today, when many people focus solely on the physical aspects of life, people who claim to have no faith frequently turn to prayer in moments of crisis. This shows that at heart we are all spiritual beings and seek a spiritual element in our lives.

You don't need a crystal or anything else when you're praying to Spirit. However, a crystal can make the prayer more effective in every way. If you touch or hold a crystal while praying, you'll find that its energy will affect the molecular structure of your body, enabling you to relate to spiritual beings on the same wavelength as your crystal. Prayer is available to everyone. People of all traditions— and even those who have no faith—pray on occasion. It's a universal spiritual language.

You can pray anywhere, at any time. You don't need to visit a church or kneel beside your bed. You can pray while waiting in line at the supermarket, while having a bath, while waiting for the traffic lights to change, or while walking the dog. A prayer is a conversation with God, the Creator, the Source, the Universal Life Force, the Infinite. It is communicating with the Divine. A prayer is the language of the soul. The more you pray, the closer you'll get to God.

Here's a prayer ritual that will give you immediate benefits. The exchange of energy between you and the Divine will have a positive effect on every cell of your body, producing feelings of happiness and well-being.

Required: a sacred space, small table, white candle, crystal, container of water, and small container of salt.

1. The first stage is to create a magic circle around the table you'll be using as an altar. You can mark the circle with a length of cord, physical objects, or candles at the four quarters of the circle. If you wish, you can visualize an imaginary circle. Place the candle, crystal, water, and salt on the altar.

2. Leave the circle. If possible, have a bath or shower and change into fresh, loose-fitting clothing. If you're unable to do this, wash your face and hands before starting the ritual.

3. Step inside the circle and light the candle on your altar. Turn to face the east and visualize Archangel Raphael, who protects the eastern quarter of the circle. Turn to the south and welcome Archangel Michael. In your mind's eye, see him protecting the south. Turn to the west and visualize Archangel Gabriel looking after the west. Turn to face north and welcome Archangel Uriel. Thank them for helping you.

4. Pick up your crystal and hold it in the palm of your left hand, which is resting on the palm of your right hand. Face east and talk to Raphael, telling him that you wish to consecrate this crystal to help you gain a closer connection with the Divine. The words

you use are not as important as your intent. You might say something along the lines of "Archangel Raphael, thank you for being with me today. I am grateful to you for your help and protection. I ask you to bless this crystal, to help me gain a closer connection with the divine. Thank you." Wait until you receive a response, and then turn to the south and speak to Michael. Follow this by speaking to Gabriel and Uriel.

5. Once you've spoken to all four archangels, and received their blessing, hold your crystal to your breast for a few moments and then place it on the altar. Speak to it. "The four mighty archangels have given me their blessing. I'll now consecrate you to be my contact whenever I speak with the divine."

6. Pick up the crystal in your right hand. Say, "I now consecrate you with the element of fire." Pass the crystal through the flame of the candle. "I now consecrate you with the element of air." Pass the crystal through the smoke produced by the candle. Place the crystal on your altar. "I now consecrate you with the element of water." Dip your fingers into the container of water and sprinkle droplets onto the crystal. "I now consecrate you with the element of earth." Pick up some grains of salt and sprinkle them onto the crystal.

7. Pick up the crystal and again hold it in the palm of your left hand, which is resting in the palm of your right hand. Speak to your crystal. "Thank you for agreeing to help me. I promise to look after you to the best of my ability." Display your crystal to each of the archangels.

8. Place your crystal back on the altar in front of the candle. Thank the archangels for their help and protection. Turn back to your altar. Snuff out the candle and step outside the circle. The rite is completed.

Your crystal is now ready to help you in all your contacts with the Divine. Hold or touch the crystal each time you pray and you'll find the bond between you will become closer and closer.

Remember, when praying with your crystal, you do not necessarily need to say anything. Prayer is often quiet contemplation and thought. Rather than thinking about what you're going to say, simply hold your crystal, relax, and open your heart and mind to God. Contemplative prayer, which this is, is a mixture of meditation and standard prayer.

Your crystal will also help you pray more often. This is because each time you happen to feel or touch your crystal, it's a sign to pray. This prayer doesn't need to be long, especially if you're in the middle of a busy day at work. Something as simple as, "Thank you God for all the blessings in my life" or "Thank you Infinite Spirit for looking after me," are all that's necessary. If you have the time, you might like to silently say the Lord's Prayer, or any other prayer that you know, as it will bring you comfort.

25: COMMUNICATING WITH ANGELS AND SPIRIT GUIDES

People have been aware of the healing and sacred powers of crystals for thousands of years. The ancient Egyptians believed that crystals played an integral part in their spiritual lives. In Exodus, the second book of the Bible, Aaron, the first high priest of Israel, wore a large breastplate containing twelve large gemstones (Exodus 28:15-30). Most major religions have also considered crystals to be important.

You can encourage angelic visitations by placing your crystal on your altar or sacred space. You can dedicate your crystal to a specific angel or to any purpose for which you need angelic help.

Method One

The easiest way to establish a permanent connection with the angelic world is through this exercise.

1. Place your crystal on your left palm and rest this hand on your right palm.

2. Either out loud or silently, tell your crystal why you want to communicate with the angelic world. Talk to it about your life and your hopes and dreams for the future. Tell it everything that you feel is relevant to your goal.

3. When you've finished talking, tell the crystal that you're going to fill it with positive energy to help establish a permanent connection.

4. Visualize yourself filling the crystal with energy. Imagine a clear white light entering the top of your head and flowing through your body to your left palm. Visualize your crystal gradually becoming surrounded by the white light.

5. Pause and wait for a response. You might feel a sensation in your left palm as the crystal responds. Other possibilities include a sense of knowing, an overwhelming sensation of love, or music inside your head. Your response might be completely different, but whatever it is, you'll know that you've received a message from the angelic kingdom.

6. Rest quietly for a minute or two, thank your crystal, and carry on with your day.

Method Two

1. Sit down comfortably and hold your crystal in the palm of your left hand, which rests on the palm of your right hand. Close your eyes and take several slow, deep breaths, silently saying "Relax, relax, relax" each time you exhale.

2. Visualize the crystal in your palm, and imagine that it's growing larger and larger. It continues to grow until you can step inside it.

3. Picture yourself surrounded by your crystal. Walk around and explore the interior of your crystal. Sit down when you're ready, and enjoy the comfort and security provided by the crystal.

4. Talk to the crystal and enjoy the sound your voice makes inside the chamber. Tell the crystal that you intend to dedicate it to the angelic kingdom (or a specific angel, if you wish).

5. Wait for the crystal to respond. This will always come, as your crystal will be happy to serve as a go-between between you and the angelic realms.

6. Talk to the crystal for as long as you wish. When you're ready, picture yourself stepping out of the crystal and watching as the crystal shrinks back to its normal size.

How to Contact the Angels

Now that your crystal is dedicated, you should hold it or keep it close whenever you're communicating with the angelic realms. You should also hold it when you're praying or saying affirmations.

Here are some other ways to contact angels.

Writing a Letter

When writing a letter, it's more usual to address it to a specific angel. Michael, Raphael, Gabriel, and Uriel are the most popular angels, as they are the four great archangels.

   Required: writing paper, envelope, pen, white candle, and your crystal

1. Sit down comfortably with the writing paper in front of you. Place your crystal centered above the writing paper.

2. Sit quietly and think about what you intend to write.

3. When you feel ready, pick up your pen and start writing. Write the letter as if you're writing to an old friend. Start by telling the angel what is going on in your life. Once you've done that, write about the important people in your life, followed by your hopes and dreams. The final part of the letter is your request. Write down what you want, express your love, and sign the letter. Seal it in an envelope addressed to your angel.

4. This concludes the first part of the ritual. If possible, wait overnight before continuing with the second part. However, if the matter is urgent, wait an hour or two and then continue.

5. Find some space where you won't be interrupted. Sit down and place the candle in front of you. Light it, and then place the envelope in front of it. Place your crystal on top.

6. Close your eyes and visualize the light from the candle expanding and surrounding you. Once you sense this, ask your angel to join you. When you sense the angel's presence, open the envelope, remove the letter, and read it out loud. Once you've done this, refold the letter and place it back in its envelope. Put the envelope back on the table and place your crystal on top.

7. Sit quietly, close your eyes, and wait for your angel to respond. The response can come in a variety of ways. You may not receive a specific response, but may receive a sense that everything will be all right. You might even receive a letter in your mind. If this happens, visualize yourself opening it and reading it. The most likely response is to receive a reply clairaudiently, which describes hearing something intuitively (see the next section). There'll also be occasions when you don't receive a reply immediately. If this happens, sit quietly for a few minutes and then gradually make yourself familiar with your surroundings before opening your eyes. Carry on with your day, confident that your angel will be attending to your request and will give you an answer when the time is right.

8. No matter what response you receive from your angel, carry your crystal everywhere you go and think of your angel and your request every time you touch or see it.

Clairaudience Ritual

Clairaudience is the art of receiving messages in your mind. It's usual for people to dismiss these thoughts when they first receive them. After all, our minds provide us with messages all day long. It often takes time and practice to determine which thoughts are psychic and which are our own.

A good way to develop this talent is to pretend to have a conversation with someone you greatly admire. Hold your crystal in your left hand while doing this. Ask this person a question and think about their answer. Repeat this several times. Ask another question, but this time make no attempt to create an answer. Wait and see what comes into your mind. Your skills will develop as soon as you stop analyzing it and allow it to occur.

Here's a ritual that utilizes clairaudience.

Required: pen, paper, and your crystal.

1. Sit down in a comfortable chair with your hands in your lap, holding your crystal. Close your eyes and take several slow, deep breaths to relax your mind and body.

2. Visualize yourself surrounded in a giant bubble of pure white light. Ask your angel to join you. You can do this silently or out loud, depending on where you are.

3. When you sense that your angel is with you, you can ask them as many questions as you wish. Your angel's answers will appear in your mind.

Don't evaluate or even think about the answers until you've finished asking questions.

4. Thank the angel for the help and advice, and for the love they surround you with.

5. Take several slow deep breaths and become aware of your surroundings before opening your eyes. Stand up, stretch, and then, before you have a chance to forget them, write down all the answers your angel gave you.

6. As many times a day as you can, hold your crystal and sense the angelic presence within.

26: YOUR CRYSTAL AND ASTRAL TRAVEL

Astral travel occurs when a person's astral body temporarily separates itself from the physical body and travels free from any physical restraints. The astral body is a spiritual body that the person travels within while in the astral plane. The person leaves the physical body behind and goes wherever they want to go, and then returns to the body. Throughout the experience, the traveler is conscious, aware, and in control.

Throughout history, there have been reports of people who could perform astral travel. However, it wasn't until the end of the nineteenth century that scientists took an interest in the phenomenon. One of the first of these was Pierre Janet, a French psychiatrist. In one experiment, he put a young lady named Leonie into a hypnotic sleep and asked her to visit the Nobel Prize-winning physiologist, Charles Richet, in Paris. She suddenly said, "It is burning." Janet tried to calm her, but she came out of the trance insistently saying, "It is burning." At that exact time, Charles Richet's laboratory was on fire, and was completely destroyed (Rogo 1978, 80–81). In 1980, Dr. Stewart Twemlow of the Topeka VA Medical Centre presented a survey on astral travel at the American Psychiatric Association's convention. He reported that 85 percent of the people who had astral traveled enjoyed the experience. "Fully forty-three percent of the subjects considered it to be the greatest thing that had ever happened to them," Dr. Twemlow reported (Rogo 1983, 8).

It's not surprising that almost everyone who has experienced astral travel has wanted to do it again. Fortunately, astral travel is a skill that anyone can learn, and once you've done it, you'll be able to astral travel whenever you wish.

Your First Astral Travel

Set aside a suitable time for your first astral travel. You might decide to do it late in the evening when the rest of your family is asleep. You might wake up early and do it then. It doesn't matter when you practice, as long as you know you won't be interrupted.

Have a bath or shower before astral traveling. A teaspoon of salt dissolved in your bath will provide protection while you're traveling. Alternatively, you can protect yourself by placing a small amount of salt in each of the four major directions.

Normally, your bed is a good place to astral travel from. However, for the first few times, a recliner-type chair or a long couch is better. This is because we associate "bed" with "sleep," and it would be a shame to fall asleep while getting ready to astral travel.

The room should be at least sixty-eight degrees Fahrenheit (twenty degrees Centigrade), as you need to be comfortably warm. You should wear light, non-restrictive clothing. You might like to cover yourself with a blanket as well.

Place pen and paper nearby, so you can record what happened in as much detail as possible.

You need a purpose for each astral travel. For your first trip, a good purpose would be to leave your physical body and float a few yards from it.

1. Sit down comfortably on your recliner chair with your crystal in your left hand. Make sure your arms and legs are uncrossed. Close your eyes and tell yourself that you're going to relax completely, then leave your physical body and astral travel. Repeat this several times.

2. Squeeze your crystal for a few moments. Relax your left hand and place the crystal on your lap. Focus your attention on your left foot. Concentrate on relaxing all the toes of your left foot. Once they're relaxed, allow the relaxation to drift into your foot, and then on to your ankles, calf muscles, knees, and thighs. Once they're completely relaxed, do the same thing with your right leg and foot. Now that both legs are relaxed, allow the relaxation to drift up through your chest, down both arms, and into your neck and face.

3. Once you're completely relaxed, focus on your breathing, and pay attention to your slow, quiet, deep breaths. Become aware of the room you're in and of any outside sounds. Become aware of your consciousness. It should be peaceful and relaxed, though you're likely to have a sense of anticipation as well.

4. Think of your purpose in taking this astral trip and gently will yourself to leave your physical body. This isn't easy, as your mind must be relaxed, but also needs to exert your will to leave the physical body. Tell yourself how important this astral travel is for you, as it will enhance your life in many ways.

5. Focus on your forehead, and allow your conscious mind to gently leave your body at this point. You're likely to feel a sense of floating or sinking as this happens. You might find yourself shaking or vibrating. Some people feel as if they're being tickled. Avoid any tendency to hold yourself back. Simply go with the flow. This isn't easy to do. It's a natural response to resist in this type of situation. If you're fortunate, you'll get beyond this stage in one attempt. Most people need several attempts before they can let go and leave the physical body. (Do not give up if you get stuck at this point. Keep practicing night after night until you leave your body.)

6. You've now left your body and are floating above it. Look down and notice how quiet and peaceful your body looks. You'll also notice that your crystal is lying in your physical body's lap. Mentally tell yourself to travel to a certain corner of the room you're in. You'll find yourself there before you've had time to even think about the request. Visit the other corners as well, and notice that you can travel from corner to corner the moment you think about it.

7. Think about returning to your physical body and you'll instantly be there. There'll be a jarring sensation as you do this. As you're returning to your physical body from inside the room, the jarring effect will be slight. Sometimes, if you return to your body from far away, the return will be more violent. It's possible to avoid this by willing yourself back to the room where your physical body is, and then returning to the body.

8. You'll become aware of your crystal as soon as you return to your physical body. Squeeze it gently. Lie quietly for a minute or two, become aware of where you are, count from one to five, and open your eyes. Stretch, then get up.

Write down everything you remember as soon as possible after the astral travel. This is a good habit to get into, as over time your records will provide suggestions for future travels. Hold your crystal if you need help recovering certain details. Your crystal will have absorbed the whole experience, and will help you recapture them.

You'll probably want to astral travel again as soon as you can. Allow at least twenty-four hours between your first and second trips. Once you've become used to astral travel, you'll be able to travel as frequently as you wish.

Crystal Travel

Once you've become used to astral traveling, you might like to experiment with other methods. This method has the advantage of being extremely fast, but is suitable only for people who have already gained experience using other methods.

As with the other method, you need to have a shower or bath before the astral travel. Protect yourself, either by using salt in the bath or by placing salt in the four cardinal directions.

1. Lie on your back and place your crystal on your forehead. Place your hands by your sides.

2. Close your eyes and relax as much as you can.

3. Focus on your crystal, and visualize energy being released from it, forming a swirling cloud of energy that reaches high into the sky.

4. Take a slow, deep breath, and as you exhale, visualize yourself being drawn into the cloud and suddenly shooting upward and into wherever you planned to astral travel.

5. When the astral travel is over, visualize your physical body and you'll be instantly returned home.

6. Lie quietly for a couple of minutes before counting from one to five and opening your eyes. Remove the crystal from your forehead, stretch, and get up.

Some people prefer to do this exercise with their crystal resting on their solar plexus, rather than their forehead. Experiment and see which method works better for you.

27: RECALLING PAST LIVES

At least a quarter of the world's population believes in rein-carnation, the philosophy that says that we have each spent many previous incarnations on earth. The soul returns to earth time and time again, each time wrapped in a new physical body. Fortunately, we can't recall every detail of our past lives, as that would make it impossible to lead effective lives in this incarnation. Imagine worrying about something you did three lifetimes ago! However, all these memories are stored inside us and can be accessed if desired.

Dream Recall

One method to gain information about your past lives is to program your crystal to help you achieve this goal. Each night when going to bed, hold your crystal before placing it under your pillow, and thank it for helping you remember lost memories. As you drift off to sleep, tell yourself that you'll dream about one of your past lives and will remember it when you wake up in the morning. The best time to do this is when you're relatively worry free and not overtired. The information will come to you in your dreams. When you wake up, remain as still as you can for a few minutes and see what memories come into your mind. Record them as soon as you can, as dream memories tend to quickly disappear.

Lucid dreaming occurs when you're in a dream and become aware that you're dreaming. Most people have experienced this, but allow the dream to continue while the conscious mind returns to sleep. However, it's possible to allow the conscious mind to take control of the dream and take you anywhere you wish to go.

1. Before going to sleep, tell yourself that you'll have a lucid dream. Do this in a casual, conversational way. You might, for instance, say, "Tonight, as I dream, I'll realize that I'm dreaming and will dream of (whatever you wish)." Decide on an action you'll take during the lucid dream. Start with something small, such as becoming aware of your fingernails. You might even decide to see your crystal.

2. If you happen to wake up and feel that you're dropping straight back to sleep, tell yourself that you'll have a lucid dream. Try to recall the dream you were experiencing, and see if you can control it.

3. Once you become aware that you're lucid dreaming, tell yourself to return to one of your past lives. See where you go. You'll find you're able to move backward and forward in time in your past life, and will gradually learn everything you wanted to know about this incarnation.

4. You're always aware that you're lucid dreaming, and can return to the present whenever you wish. It's more likely that you'll be forced back to the present well before you want to. This usually happens when you experience anything that could be troubling.

This is likely to be caused by your survival instinct acting to protect you.

5. Make notes of your lucid dream when you wake up. If you do this every time you have a lucid dream you'll gradually build up a fascinating record of your past life experiences.

Far Memory

Far memory is the art of going back in time by remembering earlier and earlier memories, until you find yourself in a previous lifetime. The technique is simple, but it takes practice to achieve success.

Required: All you need is some time and your crystal.

1. Lie down comfortably somewhere where you won't be disturbed for at least thirty minutes. Hold your crystal in your left hand if you're right-handed, and in your right if you're left-handed.

2. Close your eyes and take several slow, deep breaths. Each time you exhale, say silently to yourself, "Relax, relax, relax."

3. When you feel completely relaxed, visualize an important event that occurred in the last few years, that you were involved in. It doesn't matter how you visualize it. Some people can "see" the event clearly in their minds. Others feel it, hear it, or even smell it. Visualize the scene as clearly as you can. Squeeze your crystal gently.

4. When you've relived as much as you can of this scene, let it go and think about an event that happened when you were younger than you were in the first scene. Again, picture it as clearly as you can. Gently squeeze your crystal each time you find yourself in a different event.

5. Continue going back in time, reliving an important event each time. Keep doing this until you can go no further.

6. Now that you've gone back as far as you can, think of your desire to explore one of your past lives, and see if you can go further back in time again. At this stage, one of three possibilities will occur: you may find yourself in an even earlier event in your current life, you may find yourself in a past life, or nothing at all will happen.

7. If you found yourself in an earlier event in your current life, you can repeat step 6 as many times as you need to until you enter a past life. If nothing happens, return to the present and repeat the experiment again later. Not many people succeed at this on their first attempt. You may need to do it many times before you suddenly find yourself in a past life. Naturally, if you've entered a past life, you can explore it as much as you wish until you decide to return to the present.

8. Once you've uncovered a past life experience, you'll have no difficulty returning to it whenever you wish.

Instead of focusing on important events, you can remember simple, happy times, starting from, say, a week ago and gradually going back in time. Because far memory takes time and practice to master, it's a good exercise to do in bed at night. If you find yourself in a past life, you can explore it for as long as you wish and then go to sleep. If you fail to reach a past life, you'll be pleasantly relaxed and will easily drift off to sleep. It's easy to become despondent when you aren't successful right away. Few people succeed on their first attempts, and you may have to repeat this exercise many times before you suddenly find yourself in a past life. The best way to achieve success with far memory is to simply relax and enjoy the process, as it can be great fun to relive experiences from your past. If you approach these experiments in a light-hearted, carefree way, you'll soon achieve success.

28: THE ART OF SCRYING

Scrying is an ancient form of divination in which images are seen on the surface of a reflective object. Scryers traditionally use a crystal ball, though other items, such as a thumbnail, mirror, ink blots, polished black surfaces, a pond, or a glass of water are also used. Some people perform eyelid scrying by closing their eyes and gazing into their eyelids. The famous seer, Nostradamus, scryed by gazing into a large bowl of water.

Crystal Scrying

All you need for this experiment is your crystal and a white candle. Before starting to scry, think of a question you would like to have answered. Until you become skilled in the art, it's best to choose questions that are interesting, but not earth-shattering. Like most things, it takes time and practice to become a good scryer, and you're likely to make mistakes as you develop your skills.

You'll find it easier to scry in semi-darkness, with a source of light coming from behind you to illuminate your crystal.

1. Sit down on an upright chair. Place your crystal on a dark surface approximately two feet in front of you. Light the candle and place it slightly behind you on your left or right side. The light source should be dim, rather than bright. A flickering flame seems to help the process, but an ordinary light bulb produces good results too.

2. Look at your crystal and take several slow, deep breaths. Allow your body to relax. When you feel comfortably relaxed, continue looking at the crystal, and think of your question. Every now and again, your mind will start to wander. This is normal. Whenever you become aware of this, simply start thinking of your question again.

3. After a minute or two, you'll become aware of a slight fog or mist surrounding your crystal. This shows that you're entering the right meditative state to access your subconscious mind and receive an answer. Keep gazing at the crystal and the mist surrounding it.

4. The answer to your question will come in one of two ways. You may be fortunate enough to see the scenario played out as pictures on the misty background. It's more likely that the answer will come as a thought in your mind. Continue gazing at the crystal until you've heard the entire message.

5. Take five slow, deep breaths, stretch, and then get up.

People experience the scrying state in two different ways. Some people go into a trance state, similar to hypnosis, when they scry. However, others find the scrying state to be much the same as their normal waking state. This can be likened to the state they're in when they're captivated by a show or movie. There is no right or wrong way to scry. You won't discover the method that works best for you until you start experimenting.

Crystal Water Scrying

This method uses a plain glass container of water, as well as your crystal. Place your crystal on a dark surface immediately in front of the glass container.

1. Sit down on an upright chair approximately two feet from your crystal, with a dim light on one side behind you.

2. Take five slow, deep breaths, allowing your body to relax with each exhalation. When you feel completely relaxed, gaze at your crystal and the water-filled glass bottle behind it. Think about your question and your desire for an answer.

3. After a minute or two, you'll notice a change in the glass container. It might seem to disappear altogether, and the answer to the question will be acted out in the area the container was previously in. You might notice a mist around the container, and see visions inside it. The visions usually appear as still pictures, and there are often lengthy gaps between them. The answer can also appear as a thought in your mind.

4. Once you've received the answer, take five slow, deep breaths, stretch, and get up.

Collective Scrying

It can be a fascinating experience when two or more people scry together. This works best when both scryers are proficient at the art. The people involved sit side by side, about two feet away from the crystal. The lighting comes from either the left-hand side of the person on the left, or the right-hand side of the person on the right. The answer to the question should be of equal importance to both scryers.

The scryers gaze at the crystal until each has received an answer to the question. After the scrying session is over and the two people have had a chance to relax, they can compare notes. They'll find they each received the same answer, but if the answer came in the form of visions, they'll have seen slightly different images.

29: AUTOMATIC WRITING

Automatic writing is produced when the writer is in an altered state of consciousness. The writer records words that have not come from their conscious mind. These words have been attributed to a variety of sources, including deceased relatives, angels, spirit guides, non-physical entities, and highly evolved discarnate spirits. Many people today still use automatic writing to contact the spirit world, but it's more likely that the information comes from the writer's subconscious mind.

The process of automatic writing is simple, but it takes time to become good at it. Most people produce nothing more than circles and lines when they first experiment with automatic writing. However, with practice, words, sentences, and even books can be produced by automatic writing.

How to Practice Automatic Writing

Required: a large sketch pad and a pen or pencil with soft lead

Set a time limit for your first experiments. Ten minutes is probably enough initially, as you want to avoid boredom. Once you've gained proficiency, you'll find you can write for long periods without any sign of exhaustion.

1. Sit down at a table and place the sketch pad in front of your writing hand. Pick up the pencil and place its point on the sketch pad. Hold it in your hand as if you were about to write a letter. Your wrist must

not rest on the table, which means your hand is the only part of your body that holds the pencil against the paper. The hand becomes tired when the wrist is held away from the table. This encourages it to move and causes the pencil to write.

2. After the pencil has been placed against the paper, you need to distract your thoughts to enable the pencil to write what it wishes. This is not easy to do. We all have about sixty thousand thoughts a day, and it's difficult to suddenly stop thinking. Rather than stop thinking entirely, you could silently say a poem or something else that you learned when young, anything you can recite automatically. Once you've become experienced at automatic writing, you'll find you can distract yourself by talking with a friend, reading a book, or even watching television, as they all take attention away from the process. However, as these create additional distractions to the novice, you should avoid using them until you've gained some experience.

3. Stop when your hand gets tired, or when the time you set is up.

Most people find it hard to distract their thoughts when they first attempt automatic writing. Here are three ways to help resolve this problem.

Crystal 1

Place your crystal on the writing surface above the sketch pad. Place the point of your pencil on your sketch pad, holding it in your hand, with your wrist above the sketch pad.

Gaze at your crystal, while relaxing your body and mind. Ignore the pencil and focus solely on your crystal. After a few minutes, you may sense that the hand holding the pencil is moving. Ignore this and continue gazing into the crystal. Keep doing this until you realize that the pencil has stopped moving.

Place the pencil down and look at what you've produced.

Crystal 2

Place your crystal on the writing surface above your sketchpad, and hold the pencil in the hand you'll be using for automatic writing.

Gaze at your crystal and take several slow, deep breaths to help you relax. Continue gazing at the crystal and gently dismiss any extraneous thoughts that come into your mind. When your eyes start feeling heavy, ask your crystal what it would like to tell you. As soon as something appears in your mind, start writing it down on the sketch pad using the arm and pen you use for automatic writing. Pay no attention to what you're writing and continue gazing into the crystal. Write for as long as you wish, and stop with the tip of your pencil in contact with the paper.

Continue looking at the crystal. As your writing arm has become used to writing, you may find that it starts writing again without any input from you. Wait until it has stopped moving before placing the pencil down and looking at the results.

Circles

Another useful way to distract your mind is to draw an oval shape on your sketch pad. When you're in position, start moving your pencil in a circular motion, creating a large oval on the pad. Continue drawing around this original shape, without looking at what you're producing. Gradually allow the pencil to move inward. In practice, this usually happens automatically as the hand tires. At some stage during this process you may feel that your pencil is creating shapes or words. Stop when this sensation finishes, and examine the results.

The circles experiment can be combined with one of the crystal ones, if you wish. Place your crystal on the writing surface above your sketchpad and hold the pencil in the hand you'll be using for automatic writing. Gaze at your crystal while drawing an oval shape on the pad. Continue drawing around the first oval and continue staring at the crystal even when your hand tires and moves inward. Resist any temptation to look at what the pencil is producing until it has stopped moving.

Helpful Hints

1. Try to practice in the same place, at about the same time every day. It's a good idea to practice late in the evening when you're starting to feel drowsy.

2. You may find it helpful to hold the pencil in a different way—maybe in an open hand, or between the first and second fingers.

3. It can be helpful to try automatic writing with your less dominant hand. Some people receive better results when they do this. With practice, everyone can write with the opposite hand, although the minor hand often records the messages in mirror writing.

4. It's a positive sign to feel a tingling sensation in your arm or hand. This is a sign that you're about to receive a message.

5. Messages produced by automatic writing are generally larger than the person's normal handwriting. As automatic writing is usually produced more rapidly than normal handwriting, words are sometimes joined together and the spelling may not be as good as the person might expect.

6. The message may appear in verse, a foreign language, in mirror writing, diagonally across the page, or in an archaic language.

7. Many people find it helpful to meditate or sit quietly for several minutes before starting to produce automatic writing.

8. Be patient. It takes time to become a good automatist (the name used to depict someone who is a competent automatic writer).

30: DOWSING WITH YOUR CRYSTAL

Dowsing is the art of finding missing or hidden objects. It is sometimes confused with scrying. Scryers gaze into a crystal or some other object, in order to divine the future or find answers to their questions, while dowsers use a device, such as a forked stick or pendulum, to find missing or hidden objects. Some people, sometimes referred to as "hand tremblers," are able to dowse using their body or hands.

A pendulum is a small weight suspended on a piece of chain, cord, or thread. Wedding rings, keys, buttons, and beads are commonly used as weights for pendulums. A small piece of crystal attached to a chain or thread is another example. I wear a small piece of green jade around my neck as an amulet, and it serves as a pendulum when I need one. I know several people who wear crystal pendants that can be used as impromptu pendulums. In fact, any small weight can be used. Ideally, it should weigh about three ounces and be spherical in shape. Other shapes can be used, but rounded ones are more sensitive and easier to use.

Pendulums are readily available online and at new age stores. I prefer to buy them from a store or market, as I can experiment with them and choose the one that works best for me.

How to Operate a Crystal Pendulum

If you haven't used a pendulum before, practice on your own until you feel comfortable using it. Sit down at a table with the thread or chain of your pendulum held between the thumb and first finger of your right hand (left hand if you're left-handed). Rest the elbow of the hand you're using on the table, and allow the pendulum to dangle about an inch above the tabletop. The palm of your hand should face downward, and the pendulum should hang about a foot in front of you. Make sure that your arms and legs are uncrossed, as this closes off the pendulum.

Swing the pendulum gently back and forth until you're familiar with the movement. Allow it to swing in different directions, and then deliberately swing it in gentle circles.

While you're doing this, hold the thread at different lengths to see if the pendulum moves more easily when held in different places. Most people find the best length is between four and five inches. Experiment, though, as you may find a shorter or longer length works better for you.

When you've become used to the feel of the pendulum, stop the movements of the weight with your free hand. Once it's still, ask your pendulum which movement indicates a positive (or "yes") response. You can ask the question silently or out loud. You may find that the pendulum will immediately start moving and provide the answer. It's more likely to take time to answer. It may move slightly at first, but if you keep thinking "yes," it will gradually start moving more and more strongly.

Don't worry if it takes time to respond. Once you become used to working with a pendulum, the answers will come almost as soon as you ask them. Consequently, it doesn't matter if it takes you five seconds, thirty minutes, or even a week to learn how to use it. Everyone can use a pendulum. Some people need to suspend their disbelief before being able to use it, but it is a skill everyone can learn.

Once you have your "yes" answer, you can ask your pendulum to provide you with the other answers: "no," "I don't know," and "I don't want to answer."

Your pendulum can move in four directions: backward, forward, and side to side. It can also swing in a circle, either clockwise or counterclockwise.

The four responses you get will probably remain the same for the rest of your life. However, they *can* change. If you haven't used your pendulum for a while, you should ask for the four responses again, just in case they've changed.

The next step is to ask questions. Start with questions that you already know the answers to, as this will provide confirmation of your pendulum's accuracy. You might ask, "Am I thirty-eight years old?" If you are, your pendulum should answer "yes." If you're not, the answer should be "no." Continue asking questions about your name, age, gender, marital status, number of children, and so on, until you've become used to the movements of the pendulum, and have established how accurate it is.

The next stage is to start asking questions that you would like to have answered. Your pendulum will be able to answer these, as it can tap into your subconscious mind and bring the answers back to your conscious mind.

There is no limit to the type of questions you can ask. However, you need to remain aware that you can override the movements of your pendulum with your will. Let's assume, for example, that someone close to you is pregnant and you hope the baby will be a girl. When you ask the pendulum, "Will the baby be a girl?" it will reflect your innermost feelings and give you a positive answer, even if that is not the case.

Consequently, whenever you have an emotional involvement in the outcome, it's better to ask someone who has no interest in the outcome to hold the pendulum for you.

The pendulum is a serious instrument, and you should use it only for good purposes. It should never be used frivolously.

What Can a Pendulum Be Used For?

Pendulums can be used for a variety of purposes, including:

- Prospecting for water, oil, metal, or anything else

- Finding lost objects (Where are my car keys? Are they in the kitchen? The bedroom? Etc.)

- Finding missing people or pets (Where has our cat gone?)

- Answering any question that has a yes or no answer (Should I go on vacation in July?)

- Making an important decision (Should I accept the job offer in New York?)

- Determining your innermost feelings on different subjects (Should I have a baby?)

- Determining your probability of success (Will I be able to complete my degree?)

Why Use a Crystal Pendulum?

Pendulums are made from a wide variety of materials, such as wood, metal, and plastic. They all serve useful purposes, but a crystal pendulum contains a quality that other pendulums miss out on.

A crystal pendulum can be programmed for whatever task you wish. If you were seeking something that you'd lost, for instance, you could program your crystal to help you find it. You can also program it to contact Spirit or your higher self.

Pendulum and Crystal

You don't necessarily need to incorporate your crystal into the pendulum. Many dowsers claim that they get better results by holding the pendulum in their dominant hand and the crystal in the other. This enables them to use any pendulum they wish, while still gaining all the benefits that the crystal provides.

31: MEMORY AND YOUR CRYSTAL

Life as we know it couldn't exist without memory. Every day we need to remember names, places, facts, and even where we put our car keys. Older people sometimes blame memory faults on their age, but even children can be forgetful and absentminded. Much of the time, forgetting something can be attributed to failing to hear something correctly in the first place, or not giving the new information our full attention. If you meet someone and don't hear their name properly, it shouldn't be surprising that you don't remember it next time you meet. If you'd heard the name properly in the first place, and maybe repeated it to yourself a few times, chances are you would have remembered it. Similarly, if you put the car keys down while thinking about something else, you probably won't remember where you left them. If you'd said to yourself, "I'm putting the keys on the bookcase," you'd have had no difficulty remembering where they were.

In both examples, a few seconds of concentration would have fixed the memory in your mind. I find it helpful to touch my crystal when deliberately creating a memory. If I can't recall the information later, simply touching my crystal is usually enough to bring the information back into my mind.

Have you ever said, "I can't learn a foreign language," or "I'm hopeless at remembering people's names"? If you keep saying these things to yourself, they'll be true. When I was in high school, a teacher told me I was hopeless at French. I believed that for thirty years. It was only when I started traveling frequently that I discovered I was good at learning languages. My whole life might have been different if the teacher had said something encouraging, rather than putting me down. Consequently, if you catch yourself thinking negative thoughts, turn them around as quickly as you can. Hold your crystal tightly and tell yourself that you have an excellent memory. This is true: you have a perfect memory. Everything you've ever learned is stored in your brain. However, sometimes the recall is faulty.

Therefore, you can sometimes meet someone by chance and be unable to remember their name. As soon as you say goodbye and go on your way, the name will pop into your mind. It was there all along, but because you were frantically trying to recall it, you became stressed and the information was temporarily lost. As soon as you relaxed, the information appeared in your mind.

If you let it, your crystal will help you overcome faulty recall. Place your crystal somewhere that you can see it while you're studying something that you need to remember. Carry the crystal around with you and touch it at spare moments during the day. Test yourself on how much you remember. The use of repetition and combining the recall with your crystal will let you learn and retain new knowledge much more quickly than ever before.

Repetition is essential if you want new information to remain in your long-term memory. I find it helpful to jot down the main points about the information. Writing it down forces me to decide on the most important aspects of the material. I then hold my crystal while thinking about what I've written down, and I turn all the important points into pictures or short cartoon stories. This adds fun to the memorization, and the more ridiculous the pictures are, the easier they are to recall later. I finally add repetition by going for walks while holding my crystal, and recalling the information I've learned. I've used this process to learn speeches, jokes, foreign vocabulary, rituals, and a variety of other things that I needed to remember.

Many years ago, an acquaintance tried to recruit me into a multi-level organization he was involved in. On my second visit, I greeted everyone by name. However, no one remembered mine. It made me realize that in the minds of the organizers I was simply a number, and scarcely existed as a person. I never went back. That shows how important it is to pay attention to people's names.

Your crystal can also help you remember people's names. Obviously, the most important thing is to hear the name properly in the first place. No one will be annoyed if you ask them to repeat their name. Use their name a few times during the conversation, and repeat it silently to yourself as many times as you feel necessary. Later, maybe while lying in bed, hold your crystal and picture the people you've met. Visualize yourself addressing them by name when you next meet. Repeat this, with your crystal, at odd times during the next few days, and—if necessary—over the next week or two. This is useful for meeting one or two people, but really comes into its own if you join a new group or organization and suddenly need to learn many names.

32: MAKING EFFECTIVE AFFIRMATIONS

Affirmations are thoughts or statements that are deliberately implanted into the mind. They are said with emotion and power, as if they're already true, even though this may not be the case. Affirmations can be positive or negative. "I'm so stupid" is a negative affirmation that affirms that the person who says it is stupid. "I'm good with money" is a positive affirmation, and the person who says this frequently is likely to do well financially.

Affirmations have considerable power. People can make their lives heaven or hell depending on their self-talk. Fortunately, it's possible to change your life by changing the way you think. It won't happen overnight. If you've spent most of your life with a negative attitude, for instance, it's going to take time before you become a more positive person.

You're likely to have relapses from time to time, too. It's not easy to change from a grumpy person into someone who is constantly full of joy and light. A high school teacher I know used to be convinced that his students deliberately tried to aggravate and annoy him. Because he believed this, they did. When he tried to change his beliefs and become more positive, his students became confused and found it hard to accept the new kind person their teacher had become. Consequently, some of them acted up even more than before, and every now and again he found himself reverting to the negative person he used to be. Fortunately, his friends helped him through the process, and he's now enjoying being a teacher again.

It's perfectly natural for even the most positive of thinkers to have negative thoughts. However, instead of dwelling on them, positive thinkers notice them and let them go.

Affirmations should always be phrased as if you were already the person you want to be. Instead of saying, "I'll be happy when I finish college," for example, you should say, "I'm a happy person. My life is good."

The most effective affirmations are short. I try to make mine ten words or less. There are even one-word affirmations. "Success!" is an example. Mohammed Ali had a famous affirmation, "I am the greatest." A four-word affirmation. Even "I float like a butterfly and sting like a bee" has only ten words.

You can create affirmations for any area of your life. If there's an issue you want to work with, you might like to focus on it first, before starting on other areas. Most people I've helped with affirmations focus on confidence, self-esteem, money, or relationships before working on other areas of their lives.

Here are some examples of affirmations that you might find useful:

• I'm a confident and worthwhile person.

• I deserve the best life has to offer.

- I love and appreciate myself.

- I have a right to be here.

- I lead a life of happiness and abundance.

- I attract the right people to me.

- I love others and others love me.

- I am calm and relaxed.

- I achieve my goals.

- I'm positive and successful.

Once you've created some suitable affirmations for yourself, you need to say them as often as you can. I say affirmations to myself while waiting in line. (One I find particularly helpful in this type of situation is, "I am patient and kind.") Obviously, you can't say your affirmations out loud in this type of situation. You might be able to say them out loud when you're driving your car or you're at home. I often look at myself in the mirror while saying them. This means I can say the affirmations, hear them, and see myself saying them. I sometimes say them to myself while lying in bed at night.

Say your affirmations with as much enthusiasm as possible. I like to repeat them several times, increasing the volume each time. You can also emphasize a different word each time you say them. Say your affirmations when you're happy, when you're sad, and at any other time. Say them as if you believe them. It might be hard to believe "I live a life full of prosperity and abundance" when you're struggling to pay the rent, but in time, thanks to daily repetition, your mind will start to believe it and make it a reality. Of course, you'll have to work at achieving the goal. It's not much use affirming that you lead a life of abundance if you're not willing to do whatever is necessary to achieve it.

Your crystal can play a major part in the success of your affirmations. Make sure your crystal is in your hand or close by every time you say your affirmations. At odd times during the day, hold or fondle your crystal and silently say your affirmations to it. Whenever you feel you need more positivity, energy, or support, touch your crystal and enjoy the feelings of well-being and success it will give you.

I know people who have used affirmations to achieve their goals, but then stopped using them. Affirmations are a powerful self-development tool that you can use all the way through life to help you achieve your goals.

33: ENHANCING YOUR CREATIVITY

You are a highly creative person. Your mind is constantly providing you with ideas about every aspect of your life. You might have a talent for gardening, cake decorating, or mediating difficult situations. People sometimes think that the only people who are creative are composers, artists, and other talented people. But everyone's creative. Every time you solve a problem or come up with a new idea, you're demonstrating your creativity. Creativity is defined as the ability to create something new and useful.

You can become more creative if you want to be. There are many techniques, such as asking numerous questions, coming up with twenty solutions instead of one, spending time with like-minded people, walking in a park, doing something you don't normally do, doodling, relaxing and chatting with your subconscious mind, asking how someone you admire would do it, and thinking about the problem before falling asleep.

Everyone has experienced a sudden flash of inspiration that seemed to come from nowhere, but creativity is more, usually a four-step process. The first step is to gather information to help you come up with plenty of ideas. The second step is incubation. Step away from the problem, do something enjoyable, and allow your brain to sift through all the information you've collected. Step three is when you experience some sort of insight or "aha! moment" that provides you with the solution, or at least a path to it. The final step is to use your logical brain to perfect the initial idea and ensure that it's practical.

You can use your crystal to help you become more creative. One method I enjoy using is to write the word CREATIVE in capital letters on a sheet of paper. Place it somewhere where you can see it while you're working. Place your crystal to the left side of the first letter and start to work. When you come up with a creative idea, move the crystal onto the first letter of the word. Move it from letter to letter every time you come up with a good idea, and reward yourself once your crystal has rested on every letter. If an eight-letter word is too easy for you, try doing it with "creativity" or "I am a creative person."

Another method I use is to place my crystal in front of me when I'm doing anything creative. Each time I look at it, it reminds me of what I'm doing. If I need inspiration, I'll pick up my crystal and play with it while searching for an idea.

Your creativity is heavily influenced by your sacral chakra (about two inches below your navel). If you feel your creativity levels are not as good as they should be, or you need to increase them for any reason, you'll find this ritual helpful.

Creativity Boost Ritual

All you need is your crystal, a warm room, and some time.

1. Start by enjoying a relaxing, warm bath. Add bath salts if you wish.

2. After your bath, put on some loose-fitting clothes and lie down in a warm room.

3. Gently massage the area of your sacral chakra with your fingertips for two or three minutes. The best way to do this is to rotate your hands in small circles over and around the area of this chakra.

4. Place your crystal on your skin over your sacral chakra, and then place your arms by your sides. Think about your need for creative ideas, and ask the Divine to help you attain the degree of creativity that you need.

5. Visualize Divine energy coming into your body each time you inhale. Sense it traveling through your body and gaining power and strength in the palms of your hands and in your sacral chakra.

6. Place your hands over your crystal and visualize creative energy building up inside your crystal.

7. Hold that visualization for as long as you can, and then give thanks to the Divine for providing you with energy and creativity.

8. Lie quietly for a minute or two, then slowly count from one to five and open your eyes.

9. Eat something light and drink some water before starting on any creative activity.

You'll find that after doing this ritual your crystal will be activated. Place it where you can see it while you're working, and touch or hold it whenever your creativity needs a boost.

34: ENHANCING YOUR DREAMS

We all spend almost a third of our lives asleep. This is essential as it enables our physical bodies and conscious minds to relax and rest. However, our subconscious minds remain busy even when we're asleep, and dreaming plays an important part in that. Our dreams can transform our lives, provided we're prepared to listen to them.

Whether we remember them or not, we all dream every night. Dreams play an essential role in keeping us sane and whole. Many dreams are inconsequential and ephemeral, but some possess the power to change our lives.

How to Remember Your Dreams

Many people say that they never dream, as they can't remember their dreams when they wake up. This exercise will help you remember more of your dreams, no matter how few or how many you recall normally. The key factor in remembering your dreams is your intention. If you're determined to remember your dreams, with time and practice, you will. This is an exercise you can do in bed while drifting off to sleep.

1. Place your crystal under your pillow with the pointed end turned away from your head.

2. Lie down and make yourself comfortable. (I find it easiest to do the relaxation part of this exercise while lying on my back and roll onto my side or stomach after step 5.)

3. Relax each part of your body in turn. I start with my left foot, and allow it to feel totally relaxed before moving my attention to my left calf and telling it to relax, too. Once my left leg feels totally relaxed, I do the same with my right leg, and then gradually relax the muscles in my body, shoulders, each arm, neck, and head. There is no hurry with any of this. Take your time and enjoy the sensation created in each part of your body as it relaxes.

4. Once you've reached the top of your head, mentally scan your body and focus on any parts that are not fully relaxed until they let go and relax.

5. When you feel totally relaxed, tell yourself that you always remember your dreams. Repeat this three times, then allow yourself to drift off to sleep. (Many people find that they fall asleep well before reaching this stage of the exercise. If this happens to you, tell yourself that you'll remember your dreams at the start of the exercise.)

6. When you wake up, lie as still as you can and wait to see what you can recall about your dreams. Some people like to hold their crystal while remembering their dreams. I don't do this, as I prefer not to move at all until I've gained all the memories I can. Experiment to see what works best for you.

If you do this experiment regularly, you should keep a dream diary by your bed and record your dreams in it. This will become increasingly valuable to you over time. As you keep adding more and more dreams to your diary, you'll start to see patterns and themes emerging. I like to record my dreams on paper, and find that doing this often prompts further memories that I can include. I know people who record their dreams onto digital recorders. Experiment and use whichever method you prefer.

Dreaming with a Purpose

If you have a specific need or purpose in mind, you can charge your crystal in your sleep by holding it in your non-dominant hand when you go to bed. Examples of typical needs might include being able to get on with your boss, learning money management skills, getting motivation to exercise, or increasing your self-confidence. They can be as general or specific as you wish.

When you go to bed, go through the relaxation procedure in the previous exercise, and at step five, tell yourself whatever it is you need or desire. Give your crystal a slight squeeze while doing this. As you fall asleep, visualize what your life will be like once this goal has been accomplished.

Keep your crystal with you during the daytime and squeeze it slightly every now and again, as you visualize what your life will be like in the near future. Repeat this exercise regularly until your goal has been accomplished.

Lucid Dreaming

A lucid dream occurs when you realize you're dreaming while in the middle of a dream. People often wake up as soon as this occurs, while others observe and allow the dream to unfold. It's also possible to use the opportunity to direct your dream and take it wherever you wish. You might, for instance, decide to visit a loved one who lives thousands of miles away, and see how they are getting on. If you do this, you'll find you're instantly there. You might direct the dream to help you find a solution to a problem or to gain advice or insight. A lucid dream may help you resolve a situation that's going on in your life. You can revisit a difficult experience and make it more positive. You might choose to do something—anything—you enjoy. You might decide to see what it's like to fly like a bird. You could decide to communicate with an angel or your spirit guide. You might choose to drive a Ferrari or fly a jumbo jet. There's no limit to what you can see or do in a lucid dream.

With practice, you can learn to have lucid dreams. However, they don't always occur on demand; you need to be patient. Take your crystal to bed with you and hold it loosely in your non-dominant hand. Before dropping off to sleep, tell yourself that you'll experience a lucid dream. You might say, "I'll experience a lucid dream tonight." Repeat this several times. Squeeze your crystal and drift off to sleep, confident that you'll experience a lucid dream. Continue doing this every night until you achieve success.

While you're experimenting with this, you may find yourself waking up before you've had a chance to direct the dream. If this occurs, tell yourself that you'll stay inside the dream and won't wake up. You'll gradually pass this stage and start directing your dream where you want it to go. Make sure to do some enjoyable activities in your first lucid dreams, and wait for more important matters until you've gained some experience in the art.

When you wake up in the morning, gently squeeze your crystal and lie as still as you can while you relive everything that happened during your lucid dream.

35: ATTRACTING GOOD LUCK

Luck is the mysterious, apparently random force that brings good fortune or adversity into people's lives. It's unpredictable and appears to work solely by chance. Throughout history, people have tried various techniques, such as wearing lucky charms, performing divinations, or conducting rituals, to try to improve their luck.

In recent years, scientists have studied the phenomenon of luck and found that various techniques can improve people's luck. The superstitious practices of athletes, for instance, improve their luck, since they give them confidence and a sense of being in control.

Professor Lysann Damisch of the University of Cologne conducted a series of tests to see if luck can be influenced. In one experiment, she asked volunteers to bring a lucky charm with them when they came for the test. The charms were collected and taken away to be photographed, but only half of the volunteers received them back before the test began. The people who had their lucky charm with them performed better on the test, as the charm gave them confidence. Professor Damisch found that simply wishing someone "good luck" improved their results, as it created confidence (Damisch 2008).

Many scholars believe that crystals and gemstones were originally worn as amulets and charms, rather than simply for adornment. I carried a gemstone in my pocket for many years and used it as a lucky charm. I enjoyed handling it, and each time I did, it reminded me how lucky I was. I also found that on the rare occasions when I didn't have it with me, I could imagine that I had a gemstone in my pocket, and that worked too. A few years ago, a good friend gave me a piece of green jade that he'd carved and threaded on a string. This is what I've used as a lucky charm ever since. I can hold it and fondle it, exactly as I did with the stone in my pocket. If you decide to carry or wear a gemstone as a lucky charm, remember to remind yourself regularly that that is why you have it with you. I normally do this when I'm holding or fondling it.

I program my lucky crystal for general good luck. However, I know several people who want good luck in specific areas of their lives and program their good luck crystals accordingly. They might, for instance, want good luck and success in their business, career, sport, relationships, gambling, peace of mind, protection. Some even want help in eliminating anxiety and worry.

As well as wearing or carrying a lucky crystal, you need to constantly affirm that you are a lucky person, and that good things happen to you. I believe that your attitude toward life plays an important role in how lucky you become, as you become what you think about. It's the law of attraction. If you expect good things to happen, most of the time they will. Conversely, if you expect bad things to happen, they probably will. That's why I constantly remind myself that I'm wearing my greenstone pendant to attract good luck.

New Moon Ritual

The best time to charge your good luck crystal is on the night of the new moon. This is a time of new starts, and anything you start now has a good chance of progressing. You can charge your crystal at any other time, but if you have a choice, charge it on either the night of the new moon or full moon.

All you need for this ritual is your crystal and a small bell. The bell I use is about six inches long, half of which is the handle. It produces a beautiful sound that remains audible for some minutes. Choose a bell that produces a pleasant, musical sound.

1. Sit down comfortably in a straight-backed chair. Hold your crystal in your closed left hand, and place the bell on a table at your right side where you'll be able to reach it easily with your eyes closed.

2. Close your eyes and take several slow, deep breaths. Allow your mind and body to relax as you do this.

3. Pick up the bell and allow it to ring once. Focus on your breathing until the sound fades away.

4. Ring the bell again, but this time keep ringing it gently for at least a minute, longer if you can.

5. Place the bell on the table and listen to the musical sound the bell has created. Visualize the sound attracting good luck to you, and imagine you're absorbing good luck every time you inhale.

6. When the sound fades away, allow yourself to feel surrounded with peace and good luck.

7. Bring your crystal up to your lips and kiss it. Hold it in your cupped hands and gently blow good luck energy onto your crystal.

8. Give thanks to the Universal Life Force for attracting good luck to you and your crystal.

9. When you feel ready, open your eyes.

10. Your crystal is now ready to attract good luck to you. Keep it with you and thank it regularly for working so hard on your behalf.

Every day, you should hold your crystal in your hands and affirm that you are a lucky person. You might, for instance, say, "I am a lucky person. Good things happen to me every day." I find that the best time to do this is first thing in the morning, as it then works for me all day. I repeat the affirmation three times, increasing the volume and enthusiasm in my voice each time I say it.

Repeat the ritual as often as necessary, especially on the night of the new moon. Remember to thank your crystal every time you receive good luck, no matter how small it may be.

36: MONEY AND YOUR CRYSTAL

Everyone wants more money. No one ever seems to have quite enough. I know someone who tells everyone that he has enough money to last him for the next two hundred and fifty years. I'm not sure how he's going to manage to live that long, but in the meantime, he's busy making more money, probably so he can last the next three hundred years. Of course, few people are like him, and almost everyone experiences financial pressures at different times in their lives.

Many people have false beliefs about money. "Money is the root of all evil" and "Money can't buy happiness" are two common ones. The first belief comes from the Bible, in 1 Timothy 6:10, where it says, "Love of money is the root of all evil." The first two words give this saying a totally different meaning. Money is neither good nor evil. Money can't buy happiness, but it can make everyday life that much easier.

Negative thoughts about money become self-limiing beliefs that create feelings of poverty and lack. These beliefs often come from parents who expressed them in front of their children. Your thoughts about money ultimately dictate how much money you'll have. If you believe that making money will always be a struggle, it will be. Do you believe that only lucky people make money? Money is energy, and it can flow your way. Abundance can be yours, provided you believe it's possible.

With the help of your crystal, you can eliminate your negative beliefs about money and improve your financial position.

Make a list of all the things you would like to possess. These might include a house, car, jewelry, and travel. Alternatively, you might like to be promoted at work or find a better job, as these would give you a pay raise. No one is going to see your list, so you can write down anything you wish.

Required: your list, your crystal, a few dollar bills, and a sunny day.

1. Start by reading your list. Choose one object from it. Write this name on a separate sheet of paper.

2. Fold the sheet of paper and place it where it will receive the sun's rays for at least three hours. Place the dollar bills on the sheet of paper, and place your crystal on top of them.

3. Sit down a few feet in front of these, and gaze into your crystal. Think about the abundance you already have in your life (family, friends, health, job, money, and anything else that you value).

4. Close your eyes and think about your need for whatever you are asking for. Visualize yourself once you have attained it. Notice how happy you are. Imagine how thrilled your family and loved ones are with your success. Think about all the different ways your life will change once you achieve this goal. Allow yourself to enjoy these feelings for as long as you can.

5. Thank your crystal for helping you to do this.

6. Stay in front of your crystal for as long as you can. When you feel ready, get up and carry on with your day. Return to check on your crystal at least every thirty minutes until the three hours are almost up.

7. Sit down in front of your crystal again and repeat steps 3 and 4.

8. Finish the ritual by picking up your crystal and holding it in your cupped hands. Thank it for helping you achieve whatever it was you asked for.

9. Repeat the ritual regularly until you've accomplished your goal. Fondle your crystal at least once a day while thinking of your desire, and thank it each time for its help. Every morning, as soon as possible after you wake up, give thanks for all the abundance you already have. Once you've achieved the goal you chose from your list, choose something else and repeat the ritual until you achieve it, too.

Many years ago, I was taught to choose a small pebble after doing any ritual involving money. You need to carry it with you, in a different pocket than your crystal. The pebble will help attract money. Before performing the ritual again, place the pebble on a windowsill, or anywhere it will receive sunlight. Choose a new pebble after the second ritual. If you continue doing this, you'll build up a collection of pebbles that will help you attract money.

37: ATTRACTING PROSPERITY

Everyone wants to be prosperous. When I asked some friends to read this book, they all read this section first. You might be doing the same. According to the dictionary, prosperity means success, good fortune, wealth, flourishing, thriving, and abundance. In other words, everyone wants to enjoy the good things of life, and lead lives of happiness and plenty.

Fortunately, you can program your crystal to help manifest prosperity in every area of your life.

New Moon Ritual

The new moon has always been associated with new beginnings. Consequently, it's a good time to perform any ritual involving abundance and prosperity.

1. Cleanse your crystal. I usually do this by holding it under running water while thinking about prosperity and abundance.

2. Place your crystal in the moon's light for at least thirty minutes. An hour would be even better.

3. Hold the crystal in your left hand and sit down in a comfortable chair.

4. Close your eyes and take several slow, deep breaths. Allow your body to relax as much as possible.

5. Enjoy the feeling of total relaxation and start thinking in general terms about prosperity. Keep your thoughts positive, as you attract whatever you think about.

6. Think about how prosperous you already are in different areas of your life. Give thanks for your health, family, home, friends, car, and anything else you're grateful for. (I once spoke to a former prison inmate who gave thanks for the mouse that visited his cell and gave him company.) Squeeze the crystal in your hand and mentally send your gratitude to it.

7. Visualize a beam of clear light descending and entering your body through the top of your head. As you sense it, allow it to develop a color. This can be any color at all. Feel the energy of this color spreading through your body and into your crystal. This color is providing every cell of your body with positive thoughts about prosperity.

8. Feel your crystal in your hand and visualize it as your own personal prosperity magnet. You may even feel it throbbing with energy as you gently fondle it.

9. Give thanks to the universe for helping you remove all the blockages that have held you back from enjoying the rich, abundant life you deserve.

10. Squeeze your crystal tightly, and then count slowly from one to five. Open your eyes and sit quietly for a minute or two before carrying on with your day.

Carry your crystal everywhere you go, and hold or touch it whenever you get a spare moment. Each time you do this, think about the prosperity it's attracting to you.

You can add to this ritual by writing an affirmation on a piece of paper that you keep with your crystal. I keep them in a small drawstring bag that I bought from a new age store. The affirmation should relate to prosperity and abundance. Here are some examples:

"I attract prosperity into every area of my life."

"I effortlessly create prosperity and abundance in everything I do."

"I am grateful for all the prosperity and abundance I enjoy every day."

"I am surrounded by all the good things life has to offer."

"Wealth and prosperity are attracted to me."

Hold your crystal and read your affirmation, preferably out loud, three times a day. You should continue reading it, even once you know it by heart. By doing that, you're both seeing it and hearing it simultaneously. Put as much energy as you can into your affirmation. One good way of doing this is to repeat the affirmation several times, putting the emphasis on a different word each time you say it.

Prosperity Bath

This is an enjoyable way to attract prosperity into your life. You'll need some high quality, expensive bath salts, a thick, luxurious towel and bath mat, your crystal, and at least thirty uninterrupted minutes. You'll also need to dress yourself in good quality clothes (or nightgown or pajamas) after the bath. You might like to have a candle or two and play some gentle music. The idea is to surround yourself with anything that makes you feel prosperous.

Relax in the bath for as long as you wish. Hold your crystal in your hand or lay it on your chest. Give thanks for the abundance you already have in your life, and then start thinking about the future and how you'd like it to be. Say some prosperity affirmations, preferably out loud, and then close your eyes and visualize what your life will be like twelve months (or whatever period you wish) from now.

Enjoy the visualization for as long as you wish, then get out of the bath. Enjoy drying yourself with the beautiful towel and dressing in luxurious clothes.

Empty the bath, snuff out the candles, and turn off the music. Squeeze your crystal and thank it for acting as your own personal prosperity magnet.

A Home for Your Crystal

In feng shui, the wealth or prosperity area of your home is situated at the corner of your house or apartment that is diagonally to the left of your front door. This area should be well lit, as light attracts ch'i energy, which is the Universal Life Force. Ideally, this section of your home should not contain a bathroom or toilet, as running water symbolizes wealth, and in these rooms you can literally see your wealth draining away. The remedy for this is to keep the lid of your toilet down and the bathroom door closed.

When you're at home, you can keep your crystal in this part of your house to attract wealth and prosperity. You might like to create a special place for your crystal in this part of your home. Whenever you see it there, it will remind you that prosperity is being attracted into your home.

Prosperity Grid

A prosperity grid is an arrangement of coins placed around your crystal to help attract abundance and prosperity. You can create one whenever you wish. Some people make permanent prosperity grids for themselves. If you do this, make sure that the area, crystal, and coins are kept clean and free of dust.

All you need are sixteen coins (of different denominations and from different countries, if possible), a compass (I use the compass in my cell phone), and your crystal.

1. Clean an area approximately one square foot in size where you'll create your prosperity grid.

2. Gently cup your crystal in both hands and thank it for attracting prosperity into your life.

3. Place your crystal in the center of the space. Place a coin about an inch east of the crystal. Continue by placing a coin in the south, west, and north positions. Thank them for energizing your crystal.

4. Place four more coins in the east, south, west, and
   north directions, about an inch away from the coins
   you've already placed in position. Again, thank them
   for energizing your crystal.

5. Place four more coins in position in the east, south,
   west, and north. This creates four lines of coins (each
   containing three coins), which indicate the four
   cardinal directions.

At least once a day, sit in front of your prosperity grid and
gaze at your crystal while thinking thoughts of prosperity
and abundance. As your prosperity increases, you can add
additional coins to your prosperity grid.

You should also carry your crystal around with you during the day. Whenever you touch it, you will be reminded of
your goal. When you return home in the evening, you can
place the crystal in your prosperity grid overnight.

38: USING YOUR CRYSTAL FOR ENERGY, MOTIVATION, AND WILLPOWER

Have you ever sat at home, feeling exhausted and ready for a nap, when a friend called and suggested you both do something exciting? Did the exhaustion disappear in a matter of moments? The chances are that it did.

We can all summon up energy when it comes to doing something we enjoy, but there are times when we need to find the necessary energy to work on tasks that may not be particularly exciting. In a case of that sort, you also need to find a way to motivate yourself and create enough willpower to continue working at it until it's completed.

Fortunately, your crystal can give you all the energy, motivation, and willpower that you need.

Take your time when you first experiment with this ritual. Once you've mastered it, you'll be able to energize yourself in a matter of minutes.

As always, make sure that the room is reasonably warm, and that you're wearing comfortable, loose-fitting clothes. You might play meditation music to help you relax.

1. Sit down in an upright chair, with your feet flat on the ground and your hands resting on each other in your lap, palms upward, holding your crystal.

2. Close your eyes and take several slow, deep breaths, silently saying, "relax, relax, relax" each time you exhale.

Once you feel your body starting to relax, forget about your breathing and focus on relaxing every cell of your body.

3. Once you feel totally relaxed, allow yourself to enjoy the wonderful feeling for a minute or two. Then visualize a ray of brilliant red energy high above you. Imagine it coming down and entering your body through the top of your head.

4. Visualize the powerful red energy spreading to every part of your body, cleansing and revitalizing every cell. Allow this red energy to gather in your palms and surround your crystal with powerful energy.

5. Enjoy the stimulation provided by the red energy for as long as you wish. Once it fades away, visualize orange energy entering your body and spreading into every cell in the same way the red energy did. Allow it to drift into your hands and then into and around your crystal. Enjoy the sense of making the most out of every situation that the orange energy provides.

6. When you feel ready, allow the orange to fade away and replace it with a beautiful yellow energy that again descends and enters your body through the top of your head. Feel a strong sense of self-worth and confidence flow through you as the yellow energy spreads throughout your body. Sense the yellow energy surrounding and entering your crystal.

7. When the yellow dissipates and fades away, visualize pure green energy descending from the sky and entering your body. Feel a sense of love and inner peace as it spreads throughout your body. Allow these feelings to enter and surround your crystal.

8. When the green energy fades away, take a few slow, deep breaths before visualizing a cool, refreshing blue energy descending and filling you with gratitude that you can express your truth. Allow the blue energy to surround and enter your crystal.

9. Once the blue energy has faded away, visualize a beautiful indigo energy entering through your head and spreading throughout your body. Feel a sense of gratitude for your powerful imagination, intuition, and wisdom, as it moves around your body and into your palms. Sense it surrounding and entering your crystal.

10. The final color of this rainbow of energy is violet. Allow the indigo to disappear, and visualize the pure violet energy spreading throughout your body. Allow a sense of spirituality and gratitude for your powerful connection to the Divine to spread through you. As before, allow the violet energy to surround your crystal.

11. After the violet energy disappears, take a few slow deep breaths and thank the universe for filling you and your crystal with all the power, motivation, and energy that you could ever need.

12. Count slowly from one to five and open your eyes.

You now have all the motivation, vitality, and energy you need to start and complete any task. You've also filled your crystal with the same energy. Carry it with you and hold it for a few seconds whenever you need power, motivation, or energy.

With practice, you'll be able to perform this ritual, with or without your crystal, in a matter of minutes. I prefer to take my time with it, as I enjoy visualizing every cell of my body being energized by all the colors of the rainbow. However, I'm happy to perform it quickly if I need extra energy or willpower right away.

39: CRYSTAL HEALING

Crystals possess no healing power. However, they can help you focus on areas of dis-ease, and may provide energy to enable healing to take place. If you have a medical problem or are concerned about a possible problem, you should always seek professional help.

However, crystals can be useful in dealing with minor problems, such as tension, stress, headaches, and other pains. Here's an example. Recently, I was watching a game of soccer and strained my right forefinger while trying to catch a ball that was kicked into the bleachers. The initial pain disappeared quickly, but when I woke up during the night the finger was throbbing. I placed a crystal on it until the pain went away and I could get back to sleep again. I placed a crystal on the finger whenever it felt painful, for about a week, until the finger was completely healed.

You can do the same. If you have a sore neck, a tension headache, a bruise, or some other minor problem, place a crystal directly onto the area of pain and hold it there for ten minutes, or until the pain eases. Continue doing this regularly until the problem is resolved.

Healing Light

Another popular form of crystal healing involves a healing white light. You can perform this if your crystal is wand-shaped with a tip.

1. Stand with the crystal in your right hand (left if you're left-handed). Raise your other hand to shoulder level, with the palm facing upward.

2. Close your eyes and visualize an unlimited supply of white healing light entering your body through the palm of your left hand. Feel it spread throughout your body until every cell of your body is full of this white healing light.

3. Allow the white light to flow from your right palm and fingers into your crystal, filling it to overflowing with healing energy.

4. Give thanks to the architect of the universe for providing you with healing energy.

5. Open your eyes and lower your left arm. You can now point the tip of your crystal at any areas of discomfort or pain in your own body or the body of anyone else, provided you have their permission. You can also use your crystal to help alleviate pain in pets and other animals. As you focus the tip of the crystal at the problem, visualize the healing energy leaving the crystal and flowing wherever you wish it to go.

Instead of using the left hand, many people prefer to visualize the healing light entering the body through the top of their head. Experiment with this and see which method works better for you.

Emotional Healing

You can also use your crystal to help alleviate emotional problems, such as disappointment, sadness, fear, despair, and anxiety.

1. Lie down and make yourself comfortable.

2. Close your eyes and hold your crystal immediately above the top of your head. Imagine the energies of the crystal balancing and harmonizing your crown chakra.

3. When you feel ready, slowly bring the crystal down your forehead until its point is indicating your brow chakra (between your eyebrows). The crystal can make direct contact with your skin, if you wish. Alternatively, keep the tip of the crystal about one inch away from your body.

4. Keep the crystal over your brow chakra while you visualize the crystal sending healing energy to it.

5. Continue moving the crystal slowly down your body, pausing long enough at each chakra for the crystal to stimulate and energize it. Visualize this occurring.

6. Hold the crystal over the area of the root chakra for two or three minutes. This chakra keeps you rooted to the ground, and you need to feel thoroughly grounded for emotional healing to take place. Consequently, it pays to spend extra time holding your crystal over this area while visualizing your strong connection to the ground.

7. Once you've completely energized the root chakra, bring your crystal up to the area of your heart chakra and energize it once again. This chakra relates to love and emotion, and it's important that this chakra is harmonized and in balance.

8. When you feel ready, bring your crystal up your body to the brow chakra. This needs to be balanced to keep you in the everyday world.

9. Finally, hold the crystal over your crown chakra again and slowly bring it down your body to your root chakra.

10. Place the hand that's holding the crystal to your side and relax for a minute or two before opening your eyes and getting up.

11. Repeat this exercise as frequently as possible until you feel whole once again.

One Crystal Healing

You can dedicate your crystal to a specific healing task, and then wear it around your neck or carry it in a pocket or purse to ensure that you receive its healing energies wherever you happen to be.

Fondle, stroke, or hold the stone each time you become aware of it or have a minute or two to spare. While doing this, think of the healing energy the crystal is sending to you.

Cleanse and recharge your crystal regularly, and continue wearing or carrying it until you are feeling fit and well again.

Healing Others

You can use your crystal to help heal others, if they ask for your help. You must always remember, when doing this, that the healing comes from the Divine. You and your crystal are the conduits that enable the healing power to work, but you are not the healer. It's a privilege to be able to help others, but you must always acknowledge and thank the Universal Life Force for performing the healing.

40: CURING HEADACHES

It's rare to find someone who never gets a headache. More than thirty-seven million people in the United States suffer from migraines (Migraine.com), and approximately eighty percent of adults experience stress and tension headaches every now and again (WebMD).

Medical treatment is required for people who suffer from migraines or cluster headaches, but fortunately a crystal can be used to help alleviate tension headaches. These are usually caused by stress, eyestrain, dehydration, hunger, excess alcohol, bad posture, or lack of sleep.

Method One

1. Sit down comfortably, ideally somewhere where there aren't too many distractions. Hold your crystal in your left hand and place your right hand on the area of pain.

2. Take several slow, deep breaths, holding each inhalation for a few moments before exhaling.

3. Close your eyes and visualize a pure, white light coming from the Divine and surrounding you with healing energy. Feel the crystal in your left hand and imagine it being stimulated and energized by the white light. Visualize this energy passing up your left arm, traveling through your body and down your right arm and out through your hand, providing feelings of relaxation, ease, and comfort to the area that is causing pain.

4. Continue allowing the pure white light to be energized by your crystal and passed to and through the area of discomfort to your right hand, until the pain disappears.

5. If possible, sit quietly for a few minutes before carrying on with your day.

After doing this, wash your hands and the crystal with soap and water.

Method Two

1. Sit down comfortably on a straight-backed chair. Roll your shoulders several times to release any tension that has gathered there.

2. Take several slow, deep breaths, saying "relax, relax, relax" each time you exhale.

3. Pick up your crystal and close your eyes. Feel the energy of the crystal as it lies on your hand. Visualize a beam of white light coming down from the sky and filling your crystal with healing energy.

4. When you sense that your crystal is filled to overflowing with Divine energy, place it over the area of pain and hold it there while visualizing the crystal neutralizing and dissipating all the pain until the headache has completely gone.

5. If you can, sit quietly for a few minutes before carrying on with your day.

6. Wash your hands and the crystal with soap and water before doing anything else.

Method Three

1. Lie on your back on a bed or the floor. Bend your legs to provide more comfort, if necessary.

2. Hold your crystal while taking several slow, deep breaths.

3. Close your eyes and place the crystal on your brow chakra, between your eyebrows.

4. Become aware of the energy from the crystal as it stimulates your brow chakra.

5. Visualize a healing white light coming down from the sky and into your crystal. In your mind's eye, see the white light entering your body through the crystal and flowing to the areas of pain or discomfort.

6. Continue visualizing this until your headache has completely gone.

7. When you get up, wash your hands and the crystal with soap and water.

41: MAKING A CRYSTAL ELIXIR

A crystal elixir is a liquid, usually water-based, that has been charged with the energy of the crystal that was used to make it. When the elixir is used, the healing properties of the crystal are assimilated into the body to improve the person's life. Because of this, a friend of mine calls them crystal tonics, as he feels crystal elixirs act in the same way as a tonic.

There are two ways to make crystal elixirs. The first is called the *direct method*. This involves putting the crystal in direct contact with the water. It is convenient and easy, but is potentially dangerous, as many crystals contain poisons such as lead, mercury, and copper. In the second method, the crystal is not in direct contact with the water. Consequently, it is called the *indirect method*. That is the method we'll discuss here.

Required:

- Two glass containers with waterproof seals. One needs to be small enough to fit inside the other.

- One crystal

- Pure water (natural, spring, bottled, or rain)

- A liquid preservative (quality vodka, brandy, or vinegar)

- A dark-tinted glass bottle to store the elixir in

The Indirect Method

1. Start by clearly stating your intent. This is the reason why you're making the elixir.

2. Cleanse and charge your crystal. Place it inside the smaller of the two glass containers.

3. Place the small container inside the larger one.

4. Pour the water into the larger container. Seal it closed. Water should not be making direct contact with the crystal.

5. Place the containers in direct sunlight or moonlight for four to five hours.

6. Remove the smaller container containing your crystal.

7. Pour the contents of your large container into the dark-tinted bottle until it is two thirds full.

8. Fill the rest of the bottle with vodka, brandy, or vinegar to preserve it. (This is not necessary if you intend to use the elixir in the next two or three days.)

How to Use Your Elixir

You can use your elixir in a number of ways, depending on your intent or purpose when preparing it. You can use a dropper to place a few drops of the elixir under your tongue. This is an effective way to eliminate negative thoughts and to regain a positive approach to life. (If you use a pendulum, you can ask it how many drops you need.)

You can apply the elixir externally to parts of the body that need healing. You may find it beneficial to spray a small amount of the elixir on each of your chakras.

If you are administering the elixir to a pet, start by placing one or two drops into a cup of water. Naturally, large pets will need more drops than a smaller animal, but start with minute amounts and gradually increase the dosage if necessary.

You can spray the elixir onto plants to encourage growth. You can also pour the elixir onto your garden to create healthier plants.

You can add up to twenty drops of the elixir to your bath. This will relieve tension and aid relaxation.

You can make herbal tea with the elixir. (Avoid sugar and caffeine when doing this.)

You can rub a few drops of the elixir on people's foreheads to provide them with psychic protection.

Crystal elixirs can be used for space clearing too. Spray any areas of negativity with the elixir, and repeat every day until the problem has been resolved.

42: ENJOYING A CRYSTAL BATH

A crystal bath is a wonderful way to free yourself of all the stresses of the day, and to become revitalized and energized again. Set aside thirty to forty minutes to make the most of your relaxing bath.

Place your crystal in the bath before turning on the water. This enables the water to flow over the crystal and become imbued with its energy. If you wish, you can add sea salt, herbs, or other natural products to your bath. Avoid commercial bath salts or oils. Light a candle and place it where you'll be able to see it while lying in the bath.

Enjoy relaxing in the warmth of your bath. Allow the energy of the crystal water to flow through you, revitalizing and recharging every cell in your body.

Gaze into the candle flame and let your mind flow freely. Think pleasant thoughts about the past, present, and future. If you find yourself thinking anything negative, gently let it go. If you're having your bath in the evening, think about the day you've just had, starting from when you got up in the morning. Gradually move forward through the day, smiling at happy moments and letting go of anything that caused stress or discomfort. If you feel you didn't handle yourself well at any time during the day, relive the experience, but change it to show you handling the situation the way you would have liked to.

Once you've relived your day, close your eyes and take ten slow, deep breaths. Each time you inhale, visualize yourself breathing in a pure, healing white light. Each time you exhale, imagine that you're letting go of any negativity you may have in your body.

Open your eyes and enjoy being in the moment. Really see the flickering candle flame, feel the water, and sense the relaxation in every cell of your body. Tell yourself that you're a child of the universe and that this restorative bath will help you in everything you do.

Pick up your crystal and hold it in your left hand. Gaze into the candle flame again and mentally project yourself into the future. You could choose three months, five years, or any other period of time you'd like. Keep staring at the candle flame and see what comes into your mind. You might get a clear picture of what your life will be like at the time you chose. You might receive a series of thoughts that help you discover what your future life will be like. You may simply sense a feeling of what your life will be like. Keep gazing at the flame until you've received all the information you need.

Lie back in the bath and think about your future life. Are you happy with what you saw? If not, you have the power to change it.

One person I know was a computer hacker. When he did this exercise, he discovered that two years into the future he'd be in prison. That gave him a great deal to think about, and he changed the course of his life as a result. He now works in the computer security industry and is deriving great satisfaction out of using his skills for good. A woman who attended a workshop I gave told me that she saw herself with a young child when she projected herself forward. She and her partner had been trying to have a baby for a long time with no success. Once she knew she was going to have one, she relaxed and became pregnant in a matter of months.

Stay in the bath for as long as you wish. When you get out, snuff out the candle and dry your crystal before drying yourself.

You'll feel relaxed—and hopefully excited—after your crystal bath. Keep your crystal with you for the rest of the day and touch it whenever you need to relax.

Write down everything that came to you when you were looking into your future. Over the next few days, think about what you've learned. If you're happy with the future you saw, you can set some goals and start working toward achieving them. If you're not happy with what you saw, think about the changes you could make to ensure that your future life will be different.

You can have a crystal bath as often as you wish. However, choose a different period to project yourself into. Wait at least three months before having another look at a time period you've examined before. This will show you the results, positive or negative, of your thoughts, plans, and actions during the past few months.

43: ENJOYING A CRYSTAL MASSAGE

You can make any form of massage more effective by introducing a crystal. This enables you to add the power and energy of the crystal, and whatever information you have programmed into it, to the massage.

If you have learned how to massage, start in your normal way. Pause after a few minutes and hold your crystal, point downward, a few inches above the client's head. Keep it there for several seconds, and then move the crystal down until you're holding it over their feet. Again, hold it in this position for several seconds. Then move it slowly from the feet up to the top of the head along one side of their body. Move it down through the center of this person's body to the feet again, and then move the crystal slowly up the other side of their body to the top of their head.

Continue with the massage. When you feel the time is right, hold the crystal over the person's chakras one at a time, starting with the base chakra and working up the body. Hold the crystal over each chakra for about thirty seconds.

Complete massaging your client. Finish by tracing a large oval around the client with your crystal.

If you are new to massage, you might prefer this:

1. Seat your subject in a straight-backed chair. Walk around the chair in a clockwise direction, holding your crystal, point downward, in your dominant hand.

2. Hold your crystal over your subject's head for about thirty seconds.

3. Stand behind your subject and massage their shoulders. Rub and squeeze the muscles until you feel them relax.

4. Stand in front of your subject and aim the point of your crystal at each of the chakras in turn. Start with the base chakra and spend about thirty seconds on each one.

5. Continue massaging the shoulder muscles, gradually spreading your attention to the person's neck and upper back.

6. Finish by walking around the person three times with the tip of your crystal pointing down.

You can also give yourself a crystal massage if you are on your own.

1. Sit down in a straight-backed chair and hold your crystal in your cupped hands for sixty seconds. While you are doing this, visualize the crystalline energy flowing into your hands.

2. Place your crystal down and vigorously rub as much of the exposed areas of your body as you can, using both hands.

3. Stop every now and again, and repeat step one to keep your hands fully charged with your crystal's energy.

4. When you're finished, sit with your crystal in your cupped hands and thank it for energizing your body.

44: HARMONIZING WATER

In a series of books called *The Hidden Messages in Water*, Dr. Masaru Emoto, a Japanese scientist, demonstrated how susceptible water is to positive and negative thoughts and words. When he photographed frozen water crystals while thinking thoughts of love, the photographs showed that the crystals had formed into beautiful shapes. When he did the same thing while thinking thoughts of hate, the photographs revealed ugly, angry shapes. His photographs show how important it is to think positive thoughts while drinking water.

This can be taken a step further by energizing the water with your crystal. Usually this is done by placing the crystal in the container of water. Unfortunately, there are some crystals that can't be used for this. These include tiger's eye, as it contains asbestos, and any stone that contains copper or lead, such as azurite and malachite.

Fortunately, there is a method that can be performed with any gemstone:

1. Fill a glass container with water, and attach the crystal to the outside of it. The best way is to attach the crystal using cotton, string, or a chain. If these are unavailable, you can attach it to the side of the glass container with a clear tape.

2. Sit down comfortably with your crystal held in your cupped hands. Close your eyes and silently speak to your crystal. Tell it that, because you want to lead a life full of energy and radiant good health, you're

wanting to use it to help you energize and harmonize water. Ask it if it will do this for you. Pause and
wait for a response from your crystal. Usually this
will come as a thought or feeling. Be patient. Sit
quietly and wait for a response. Once you've received
a response, you can continue. Thank the crystal for
all it's done for you, and how it has enriched your
life in many ways. Tell your crystal that you're going
to tie it to the outside of a container of water that
you're going to place in the sunlight for a few hours.
Thank it for harmonizing the water, and tie it to
your container.

3. Place the container in direct sunlight for three to
four hours.

4. Remove your crystal, and thank it for harmonizing
the water for you. Bless the water as you pour yourself a glass and thank it for keeping you energized
and whole. Drink the water while thinking happy
thoughts. Keep the rest of the water in a cool place.
Think kind, positive thoughts while you're drinking
it. It's a good idea to think positively whenever you
drink water.

When you do this for the first time, you might like to
prepare two containers of water. Treat one container with
your crystal, but do nothing with the other container. After
drinking a glass of the treated water, drink some water from
the other container and taste the difference between them.

You can also experiment by taping an affirmation to the outside of your water container. Place it, and another container of water that does not contain an affirmation, in the sun for a few hours. Try them both, and see which one contains more power and energy.

Problem Solving with Harmonized Water

This is an interesting way to provide answers to questions and to resolve problems. Before going to bed, pour yourself a small glass of harmonized water. Think about your problem or concern while drinking about half of the water. As you prepare for sleep, tell yourself that you'll have the answer in the morning.

When you wake up, sit on the side of your bed and drink the rest of the water. Remain sitting quietly for a few minutes and see if the answer comes to you. If it doesn't, repeat the exercise every evening until it does. The first few times I did this, the answer was already in my mind when I woke up. On another occasion, I had to repeat the experiment several times before an answer came. Usually, the answer comes soon after I've drunk the rest of the water. I've learned not to be concerned if the answer doesn't come immediately, as sometimes it will appear during the day when I'm thinking about something completely unrelated to my concern.

45: YOUR CRYSTAL AND PLANT HEALTH

Crystal energy is just as useful for plants as it is for people and animals. You can test this by placing your crystal on top of the soil in a potted plant and willing it to send good health and growth to the plant. If possible, have another identical plant in a similar pot. Treat it well, but don't place a crystal on it. Evaluate the two plants after two weeks to determine the effectiveness of the crystal energy.

This process is not limited to potted plants. You can place your crystal anywhere you wish in your garden to encourage plant growth. Use your intuition to determine where you want your crystal to go. You can lay it on the surface, bury it completely, or plant one end in the soil. The crystal and the plant form a symbiotic relationship by helping and supporting each other.

If you plant from seeds, you can put your crystal with them to encourage plant growth.

Treating Unwell Plants

You can help plants that are unwell or not growing as well as they should, by placing your crystal next to them. If you suspect that the problem may be in the roots, push part of the crystal into the soil two to three inches away from the plant.

Another remedy is to strengthen the plant's bio-magnetic field. You do this by passing your crystal in clockwise circles around the plant, with the single-terminated end pointing downward. Do several rotations at a time, twice a day, until the plant is restored to health. After this, point your crystal toward the roots of the plant, and mentally send healing through the crystal to the plant.

If a branch or limb of a tree has been damaged, tie your crystal to the affected area to speed up the healing process.

Fresh Cut Flowers

Fresh cut flowers will last longer if you place your crystal in the vase. However, make sure your crystal is not affected by water before doing this.

Crystal Elixir

Your plants will benefit from being watered by a crystal elixir. This will improve their strength, growth, and color. Tell your plants what you're doing as you water them with the elixir.

46: BLESSING YOUR HOME

Many people hold a housewarming to bless and purify their new home before moving into it. This enables them to eliminate any negativity that might be in the house before they move in.

Nowadays, housewarmings are an opportunity to hold a party and give your friends a chance to see your new home. A housewarming is intended to bring good luck to the home and to everyone living in it.

In the past, a housewarming was done to honor and thank the spirits who lived in the house. The center of the home was traditionally the hearth, and the fire that was kept burning there was considered sacred. This probably originated with the ancient Greeks and Romans, as they had house gods who were worshipped at the hearth. Over the centuries, the house gods were replaced with a variety of imps, fairies, and other spirits. They all had to be honored and looked after to ensure the happiness and prosperity of the occupants. This is why the hearth and the grate had to be tidied up before people went to bed. A new log would be put on the fire, too, to keep the family spirits happy. When people moved into a new house, they would take live embers with them to start a fire in the new hearth. This was the original housewarming. It ensured their familiar spirits moved with them to continue the family's good luck.

There are many superstitions involved with moving to a new house. One of the best-known says that you should not take an old broom from one house to the next. To ensure good luck, you must buy a new broom to use in the new home.

Most people believe housewarming occurs only when you move from one home to another. Fortunately, it's never too late to bless your home. Some people decide to do this after something untoward has happened, and they feel the problem might be connected to their home. However, many people do it to make their happy home even better than it currently is. Consequently, you can bless your home whenever you wish and as often as you wish.

One easy way to bless your home every day is to thank it for everything it's doing for you every time you enter or leave the property. You can do this in a matter of seconds if you're in a hurry. However, it's a good idea to rest a hand on the building and spend time thinking of everything the house is doing for you.

You might also like to use your crystal to purify and bless your home. This is a two-part process. Before performing this ritual, you need to find a place in your home for your crystal where you'll be able to see it several times a day when you pass by it. An altar would be perfect, if you have one, but a quiet area in the house will do the job just as well. You'll also need to dedicate your crystal to removing all the negativity from your home.

1. Choose a pleasant, warm day. Open all the windows to allow as much fresh air as possible into your home.

2. Stand by the entrance of the property with your crystal held in your cupped hands. Think about the ritual you're about to start, and thank your crystal for its major part in the process. You might like to say a prayer to the Universal Life Force (or whatever you prefer to call it) before starting.

3. Enter the house through the main door and walk through each room in turn, starting with the rooms on your left. Walk around each room, staying as close to the walls as you can. As you do this, silently talk to your crystal, saying how grateful you are to it for removing all the negativity from your home.

4. Once you've taken your crystal into each room, return to the main entrance, thank your crystal again, and then place it in the area you prepared for it.

5. The first part of the ritual is over. For the next four weeks, acknowledge and thank your crystal for absorbing and neutralizing the negativity in your home.

6. After four weeks, cleanse your crystal in salt and water. Depending on your crystal, you might want to leave it in the solution overnight. On the following morning, rededicate your crystal to provide happiness, joy, and blessings for the house and everyone who lives in it.

7. This marks the start of the second stage of this ritual. Light a candle and walk through the house again with it. Make sure you light up the corners of each room. As you do this, thank the candle for providing happiness and light in your home. Once you've done this, take the candle out of the house through the main entrance and snuff it out.

8. Pick up your crystal and take it to the main entrance of the house, or the entrance to the property itself. Hold it in your cupped hands, and thank it for removing the negativity from your home, and for filling it with happiness, light, and laughter.

9. Enter the house through the main door and visit each room in turn, while silently talking to your crystal. Thank it for what it's done for you, and for the new life it's providing for everyone living in the home.

10. Finish the walk through the house at the main entrance, and then place the crystal back in the place you've prepared for it.

If you wish, you can add to the ritual. You might sprinkle salt in the corners of each room to provide protection. You might light a candle in the center of each room to provide light and love, or you might clap your hands or play music to provide stimulation.

Remember, though, that your crystal is the main participant in the ritual. Continue to notice it and thank it each time you see it. Keep the area around the crystal clean and free of dust, and enjoy the feelings of joy and happiness you'll feel whenever you're in your own home.

47: PETS AND YOUR CRYSTAL

If you've ever had a pet, you'll know how important their role is in home and family life. Crystals can be used to help your loved pets in two main ways: as an aid in healing when they're unwell, and to help open channels of communication between you and your pets. Your crystal can also provide healing for you when a pet dies.

Healing

Crystals have been used for healing purposes for thousands of years. One ancient method that is still used today is a crystal elixir (see use 43). This is water that has been charged with the qualities you imparted into the crystal. The water is then given to your pet to drink.

Another method is to impart healing energies into your crystal and then lay it on the afflicted part of your pet's body. This is not always possible, of course. If need be, you could tie the crystal around your pet's neck or place it in its bed. Sometimes your pet will not like the crystal. When this occurs, you need to impress the desired qualities into it again, and see if that produces better results. You also need to ensure that your pet doesn't accidentally swallow your gemstone or crystal.

Crystals will help the healing process, but if your pet is ill, your first stop should be your local veterinarian.

Interspecies Communication

Naturally, you communicate with your pet all the time. You speak to them, and your pet also reads your body language and voice. Very few people try to communicate with their pets telepathically, even though they've possibly experienced examples of it. Here's a common example. If you have a dog, you may think to yourself that it's time to take them for a walk. Your dog is likely to pick up on this thought and start bounding around you in a state of great excitement. In this instance, your dog has read your mind.

Here's an interesting test you can try. Stroke or pat your pet for a few minutes. When you stop, keep talking to your pet in your mind. You'll be able to see if your pet is paying attention, even if they are not looking at you. Speak to your pet as if you're having a chat with a good friend, which you effectively are. Your pet is highly intelligent and will resent it if you talk down to them. Tell your pet how much you love them, and how important they are to you. Talk about the day you've just had, and maybe mention one or two activities you and your pet did together. Sometimes, after communicating telepathically with your pet, they will come over and rub against you or do something else to express love and affection.

You may have to experiment several times before your pet makes it obvious that they are listening to your telepathic messages. Once you've succeeded at this, you can take it a step further. Program your crystal to help you and your pet communicate more effectively, and place it on the ground halfway between you.

Send telepathic thoughts to your pet, and continue doing so until you're sure your pet is listening. Tell your pet what you would like them to do. This is much more effective than saying the opposite. If you're asking your pet to stop doing something enjoyable, they might stop listening or even walk away. If your pet is reluctant to agree to your request, you'll have to do it again, this time looking directly into your pet's eyes. You may need to hold your pet's head to do this. After making your request, ask your pet for a response. This may come as a sense of knowing in your mind, or maybe you'll receive a friendly lick. Once your pet has agreed to your request, you can be assured that they will obey it most of the time.

Communication can't occur unless both parties contribute. Consequently, whenever you and your pet are enjoying quality time together, you need to be alert for any telepathic messages they are sending you.

Death

The death of a much-loved pet is an event that affects the whole family, and a ritual that recognizes the animal's contribution to everyone's life can help ease the grief caused by the loss.

This ritual can be performed by one person or the entire family. It can be conducted in one session, or you might prefer to spread it over a few days.

1. Spend some time in a place that was loved by your pet. It might be where their bed was, for instance, or it could be somewhere where you took them for a walk. Sit down with your crystal in your hand, and think of your love for your pet and how much you miss them. As much as possible, keep your thoughts positive. Think of happy moments you shared and funny things your pet did. Finish this part of the ritual by holding your crystal in the palms of your hands and saying (preferably out loud, but silently if necessary) how much you loved them.

2. Write a letter to your pet expressing your love, and how much they meant to you. If you wish, you can include some favorite memories of activities the two of you used to do together. Finish the letter by telling the pet how much they are missed. Seal the letter in an envelope and write your pet's name on it.

3. Place the letter in a well-lit spot that your pet knew. This might be outside in the sun, or indoors in a well-lit room. Place your crystal on top of the letter. If you are burying your pet yourself, you might place the letter and crystal on top of the casket. Leave the letter and crystal in the bright light for about

an hour to provide plenty of time for your crystal to help send your love to your pet. You can stay while this is occurring, or leave and do some other activity. If you're doing something else, try to do something that doesn't require all your attention, as you'll be thinking mainly about your pet.

4. Stand in front of your letter. Pick up the crystal and thank it for sending your love to your pet. Say good-bye to your pet in whatever way you choose. You might say a prayer or simply give thanks for their presence in your life.

5. Go outside in the early evening and burn the envelope and letter. Watch the smoke ascend and gradually disappear as it carries your message to your pet.

6. Carry your crystal with you for as long as necessary, and touch it whenever you feel upset or sad about the loss of your pet.

If you find it hard to let go, perform the rituals in chapter 10 (on how to handle grief).

48: YOUR CAR AND YOUR CRYSTAL

Driving a car is the most dangerous activity we perform in our everyday lives. We rarely think about this, though, as most people spend large amounts of time in a vehicle almost every day, as a driver or passenger. Even though cars and roads are getting safer, statistics show that motor vehicle accidents remain one of the three major causes of death for every age group.

Because of this, it makes good sense to protect your vehicle and its passengers with a crystal. After programming it to protect your car, place the crystal under the driver's seat or in the glove compartment. Secure it, to prevent it from rolling around. I keep my crystal wrapped in cotton wool inside a small box without a lid. A neighbor of mine carries her protective crystal on a keychain, to protect her when she's driving and when she's out of her car.

She also has a St. Christopher's medal hanging from her inside mirror to provide additional protection. St. Christopher is the patron saint of travelers, and over the last two thousand years, millions of these medallions and amulets have been used to provide protection for people while they were traveling.

Whenever you get into your car to drive, visualize a clear white light emerging from your crystal and surrounding the car and its occupants with a bubble of protective energy.

Think of the vehicle's wheels grounding you as they contact the road. You should also do this whenever you park the car when you're away from home.

When you're out driving, envisage the bubble of protective energy expanding to protect the road in front of and behind you. You can also send protective energy to either side, whenever you feel you need it. Interestingly, when you do this, you'll sometimes find that the drivers of cars that have been encroaching into your space will become aware of you and move back into their proper lane.

You should regularly cleanse the crystal that's protecting your vehicle. The frequency of cleansing depends on how much you use your vehicle. If you have a daily commute, you should probably cleanse your crystal at least once a week. However, if the car is used mainly for short trips in your locality, once a month should be enough. However, it's better to cleanse your crystal frequently rather than waiting until it desperately needs it.

Remove the Negativity

Every car holds a degree of negativity. This is because we all experience a variety of moods, both good and bad, when we're driving. Most people have experienced anger and aggression when someone cuts them off on the road or makes a rude gesture at them. Everyone, no matter how meek and mild they might be, has experienced some form of road rage. Some experience it almost every time they get behind the wheel. No wonder most cars are full of negative energy.

Here's a simple way to remove the negativity from your vehicle:

1. You can use a smudge stick containing sage to purify the interior of your car. Be careful, especially with the upholstery, as smudge sticks get extremely hot. An alternative to this is to beat a drum inside your car. You can even use a stick and a tin can for this, if you wish.

2. Sit in the driver's seat of your car with your crystal resting in your cupped hands. Close your eyes and visualize the crystal in your mind's eye. Thank it for agreeing to protect your car and its occupants.

3. Pause for about thirty seconds, and then ask your crystal to remove all the negativity in the car and re-place it with positive energy. Wait silently, with your eyes closed, until you receive a response. It could happen in a matter of seconds, or possibly take a few minutes. The response might come in the form of a tingling sensation in your palm, or maybe a sense of knowing that the task has been done.

4. Visualize a clear white light emanating from your crystal and filling the car with positive energy. Watch it spread beyond the car, surrounding it in a bubble of white light.

5. Repeat this procedure whenever you feel your car has been exposed to negative energy.

Relieving Anxiety and Stress

Our roads seem to be getting busier by the day. It's no wonder many people are anxious when they get behind the wheel. Some people suffer from this, no matter what road they're on, while others feel stressed only on certain roads, such as freeways, or when they're stuck in traffic.

Holding a crystal while taking slow, deep breaths is a good remedy for this. If driving anxiety occurs all the time, you should dedicate your gemstone to relieve the tension, and then place or attach it somewhere you can see it without taking your eyes off the road.

49: HAVE MORE FUN

Everyone knows that children laugh much more than adults. However, it's an urban myth that children laugh three hundred to four hundred times a day, while adults laugh fifteen to twenty. As most people laugh while interacting with others, the number of laughs per day is determined by how much contact the person has with other people. All the same, children laugh much more frequently than adults.

Of course, as an adult, it's hard to live life entirely in the present moment. People worry about something they did yesterday or the day before. They're also concerned about large bills that need to be paid in the next week or two. At the same time, they might be working on a deadline that's due today. It's hard to have fun when you're consumed with problems relating to the past, present, and future.

When was the last time you had a good belly laugh? Some people find it hard to remember the last time they had a laugh of any sort.

No matter how busy you are, you owe it to yourself and your health to have at least a few minutes of fun every day. Make a list of all the things you enjoy doing. Some of these might be major, such as traveling overseas. Others might be easy to fit into an average day. Reading a book, chatting with a friend, going for a walk, or walking barefoot in the grass are examples. If you're leading a hectic, busy life, simply spending five minutes on your own might be all that's required.

As well as the items on the list you've created, you might like to incorporate a few random, fun activities into your everyday life. Examples include spinning around in your desk chair, learning a joke and telling it to others, displaying a fun saying in your office, and performing a random act of kindness.

You can program your crystal to make you feel happy and full of fun whenever you hold it. Here's a ritual to help you do that.

Choose a place that you're not familiar with to perform this ritual in. You might choose a quiet spot in a nearby park. If you enjoy being in a busy environment, you might choose a coffee shop that you haven't visited before. It makes no difference where it is, and no one will know what you're doing. The important thing is that you feel comfortable and safe. The purpose of going somewhere new is to take you out of your comfort zone.

1. Become familiar with the setting you chose.

2. Hold your crystal and think of a time when you laughed and felt full of the joys of life. It doesn't matter when this time was. You might choose an incident that happened when you were five years old. It could be something that happened last week. Smile as you relive the experience.

3. Let that memory go and think of your life as it is now. See how many humorous thoughts come into your mind. Think about your need to have more fun in your life.

4. Mentally go through the list you wrote of all the things you enjoy doing. Decide on one that you can do today. Imagine yourself doing whatever it is, and allow feelings of fun and laughter to come into your mind. Hold these thoughts for as long as you can, while gently stroking your crystal.

5. Resolve to do a fun activity every single day.

6. Get up and carry on with your day. Feel excited whenever you think about the fun activity you'll be doing later. If your fun activity involves others, you may have to contact them to see if they're available, and to arrange a suitable time.

7. Finally, it's time to do the fun activity. Fondle your crystal before starting whatever it is. Enjoy the activity. Deliberately discard any thoughts about the past and future that come into your mind. Focus on the present and obtain as much pleasure as you can from your fun activity.

8. Later, fondle your crystal and relive the activity in your mind as you drift off to sleep.

Make sure to repeat this exercise until you're automatically including at least one fun activity into your life every day.

50: THE CRYSTAL SÉANCE

This séance is designed to eliminate all forms of negativity, while enhancing a positive approach to life. You can conduct it with as many like-minded people as you wish, or, if you prefer, you can conduct it on your own.

All you need is your crystal, a few towels, a bowl of water, and a table. The séance can be conducted in full light, though some people prefer to do it in semi-darkness. Ideally, the séance should be performed in pleasant surroundings, either indoors or outdoors. You can add atmosphere by using lit candles and flowers. Pleasant meditation music, sounds of nature, or a quiet, slow-moving classical piece will help too.

Place the bowl of water in the center of a table. Place the towel beside it and lay your crystal on top. Place as many chairs as necessary around the table. If you have too many people to fit around your table, place the bowl on the floor and have everyone sit on cushions around it.

Choose your guests carefully. When you invite them, tell them that they'll be participating in a séance to eliminate negativity, and ask if they would be interested in attending. If they express interest, tell them to think of something negative they'd like to eliminate from their lives, and say you'll be attempting to banish it. Your guests don't need to tell anyone what the negativity is. Your guests don't need to be true believers, but they must be open-minded about the idea of a crystal séance.

The séance can't begin until all your guests have arrived. Welcome them and offer them something to eat and drink. Try to keep the conversation as light and happy as possible. Séances always work better when people approach them in a positive, happy state of mind, as everyone releases tension during the proceedings.

Once everyone has arrived, ask them to sit around the table and tell them what's going to happen. You might say, "We're here today for a special purpose. It's time to release all the unwanted negativity that we carry inside us. The negativity might be a bad habit, such as smoking. It could be feelings of guilt. It might be jealousies, or an inability to forgive. It doesn't matter what the negativity is. Today we're going to eliminate all the negativity from our lives, replace it with powerful, positive energy, and start again as confident, happy people.

"One by one, we're going to hold the crystal in our cupped hands and empty all our negativity into it. The empty space in our hearts will be filled with vibrant, positive energy. Once this has been done, the crystal will be washed in water to eliminate all the negativity.

"The person who placed the crystal in the water will then remove it, dry it and wrap it inside this towel. Then pass it on to the next person. We'll continue doing this until everyone has had a turn."

Pick up the crystal and hand it to the first person. Guide them through the exercise, if necessary. Allow the person as much time as necessary to release their negativity. Once this person has finished, they will place the crystal in the water, bring it out again, dry it, and pass it, wrapped in the towel, to the next person.

After everyone, including you, has had a turn, everyone closes their eyes and says a silent prayer. After this, you take the crystal out of the water and dry it for the last time.

"While we're all here together," you say, "Let's use the opportunity to send peace to all the world. On the count of three, I'll say, 'What do we want?' and you'll reply, 'We want peace in the world.' We'll say it three times."

Smile at the group and say, "What do we want?"

"We want peace in the world."

This is done three times. Once they've done it, say, "Thank you. Go in peace."

This doesn't complete the séance. Encourage everyone to talk about their experience and how they felt before, during, and after the séance. This finishes the séance on a positive note, and everyone will go home feeling happy and positive. You're likely to find one or two of your guests will ask if they can attend next time you perform the crystal séance.

Afterward, you'll need to dispose of the water. As you pour it away, express your gratitude to it for absorbing everyone's negativity. Wash the bowl thoroughly before using it for any other purpose.

You can perform this ritual by yourself, whenever you wish. After you eliminate the negativity, send love, joy, and happiness to anyone you wish. It could be an individual, people who care for others, or maybe everyone in the world. The whole universe will benefit from your positive thoughts.

You can perform this séance as often as you wish. One thing I particularly enjoy about this séance is that it can be done anywhere, provided you have your crystal with you. It's usually easy to find a container for the water.

If you're presenting this to a large group of people, you'll be able to speed up the proceedings if you remove the crystal from the bowl and dry it before handing it to the next person.

An interesting variation of this séance is to hand everyone a sheet of paper and ask them to write down the negativity they want to release. These slips of paper are folded and kept by each participant. When it's the first person's turn, they place the crystal on the table in front of them, and then open their piece of paper and silently read what is written on it. They then tear the paper into tiny pieces, which are placed in their left palm. The person picks up the crystal and places it on top of the pieces of paper, before covering it with the palm of their right hand.

The person silently thanks the crystal for absorbing all the negativity. The crystal is then placed in the bowl of water, followed by the tiny pieces of paper, which provide evidence that the negativity has been destroyed.

CONCLUSION

I hope you've tried experimenting with many of the ideas in this book and are now as addicted to crystals and gemstones as I am.

While reading this book, you may have encountered people who said that you can't do certain things with the crystal you own. Of course you can't, if you feel that way. For example, years ago, an acquaintance read me a passage from a book on crystals that said rose quartz was the only stone that attracted love. She was convinced that she hadn't attracted a partner because she'd been wasting her time using the wrong stone. I suggested she ask her intuition if her stone could be used to attract love. Much to her surprise, she found it could. Eventually, she found the right partner, and they've been happily married for many years. The lesson I learned from that experience is that you should trust your intuition rather than what a book—even this one—might say.

Consequently, don't accept everything in this book on face value. Experiment, test, have fun with your crystal, and make up your own mind. Read as much as you can, and use your intuition on every crystal you come across.

APPENDIX A:
STONE SUGGESTIONS

Most people become interested in crystals after receiving one. They may have been given it, found it unexpectedly in a store, or obtained it in some other way. No matter how the stone came into their possession, chances are that it marked the start of a collection, as few people can stop with just one crystal.

Here are some suggestions for stones that you might like to add to your collection.

Agate (Variety of Colors)

The Egyptians were mining agate as far back as 3500 BCE, showing how long it has been valued and cherished. Agates are grounding stones that help people realize their true worth. They protect pregnant women, before and after childbirth. They also provide protection for travelers and give strength to people involved in physical work.

Moss agate has always been valued by gardeners, botanists, and anyone else working on the land, as it has branched markings that look like moss covering the surface of the stone. It is a stone of wealth and prosperity, as it attracts abundance in the garden, and in every other area of life.

Amethyst (Violet)

The ancient Egyptians believed that anyone wearing an amethyst could not get drunk. The Greeks shared this belief, and called the stone *amethustos*, which means "not drunken." It is also said to provide relief from insomnia and headaches. Amethyst has a calming effect on the mind and is often used for meditation. Amethyst enhances spiritual awareness and psychic perception. It also dispels any negative energies.

Aventurine (Green)

Aventurine is a variety of quartz. It is usually green, but is also found in blue, brown, orange, and red. It has always been considered a lucky crystal. Aventurine helps create wealth and provides good luck in anything involving chance or a calculated risk. It provides luck in many small ways, too, such as a chance meeting or a career opportunity. The name aventurine comes from the Italian word *a ventura*, which means "by chance."

Aventurine is a positive stone that creates feelings of health and vitality, and provides help in every area of life.

Bloodstone (Dark Green with Red Streaks)

Over the last few thousand years, bloodstone has had several names. It was originally called heliotrope, which is derived from two Greek words that mean sun-turner. They believed the gem could alter the rays of the sun, making them appear red. It has also been called jasper. According to Christian legend, there was green jasper at the foot of the cross when Jesus was crucified. Drops from the blood of Jesus dropped onto the jasper, creating bloodstone, the dark green gem with red spots that we know today.

Bloodstone provides courage and strength. It eliminates emotional stress and purifies the blood. It is often used to provide protection, especially for travelers.

Carnelian (Brownish-Red to Salmon)

Carnelian provides courage, leadership, ambition, and persistence. Speakers wear it to provide them with confidence and eloquence. Carnelian is a motivating stone that keeps people grounded and focused on their goals. It was traditionally worn to attract love and passion.

Citrine (Golden Yellow)

Citrine is a yellow stone, and its name is derived from the French word *citron*, which means lemon. It's known as the "merchants' stone" or the "money stone," as it's believed to bring prosperity and energy to whomever owns it. Citrine is good for self-esteem and enables you to express yourself clearly in words and on paper. It also enhances creativity. It is a happy stone that encourages forward-thinking.

Fluorite (Violet)

Fluorite is one of the most popular stones in the world. It is sometimes referred to as the "genius stone," as it enhances learning, memory, and problem-solving. It stimulates the third eye chakra, enabling people to understand how they think.

Purple Fluorite relates to meditation, spirituality, and intuition. It is also a stone of protection, and this protection is thought to increase the longer the stone is used. Fluorite also protects people from bad dreams.

Hematite (Gray to Black)

Hematite is known as the "stone that bleeds," as it gains a reddish streak when rubbed against a touch stone. The word hematite comes from the Greek *haima*, which means blood. Greek soldiers wet the stone and rubbed it on their bodies to provide protection in battle.

Hematite stimulates the blood and the circulatory system. It's a grounding stone that creates balance and eliminates negative thoughts. It also aids sleep if placed under the pillow.

Red Jasper

Jasper is available in a wide range of colors. It has been used for protective purposes for thousands of years. Red jasper is called the "stone of endurance," as it encourages people to persevere until the task is completed.

Red jasper calms the mind and alleviates stress. It protects people who perform physical work. It has a strong spiritual element, which provides great focus when communicating with the Divine.

Labradorite

Labradorite was discovered in Labrador, Canada, in 1770. It is a blue-gray opalescent crystal that is popular because, after it's been cut and polished, its characteristic iridescence, known as labradorescence, produces flashes of green, blue, red, and violet rays across its surface. This makes it one of the most fascinating of all stones. Labradorite increases people's innate psychic and spiritual abilities. It balances conflicting emotions and aids in self-understanding. It also reminds people not to overlook their special talents and skills.

Lapis Lazuli (Deep Blue)

Lapis Lazuli has been sought after throughout history because of its vivid blue color. The gold flecks that can be seen in lapis lazuli made it a popular stone for royalty and other people of importance. The sarcophagus of King

Tutankhamen was inlaid with lapis lazuli. Lapis lazuli has always been considered a symbol of wisdom, honesty, and spirituality. Lapis lazuli provides courage and wards off negativity. It helps people become the very best that they can.

Malachite (Green)

The Egyptians were fascinated with malachite and started mining it six thousand years ago. The ancient Greeks and Romans also used it for jewelry and decoration. They also ground it into powder to make eye shadow.

Malachite has always been considered a powerful healing stone. It absorbs negative energies and is useful in eliminating any harmful rays from technological equipment. It protects long distance travelers and people who work in the travel industry.

Peridot (Green)

Peridot is one of the few gems that appears in only one color. It has been worn for thousands of years to ward off evil forces and negativity of any form. It's still worn for this, but nowadays it's usually worn to boost self-esteem, and to attract positivity and abundance.

Peridot is a stone of transformation and helps people overcome addictions and fears. It releases nervous tension, as well as feelings of guilt and inadequacy. If worn or carried as a lucky charm, peridot will increase laughter, eloquence, and happiness.

Clear Quartz (Clear to Milky White)

Quartz can be found all around the world and is one of the most plentiful of all stones. It comes in many forms, and many crystals better known by other names are actually quartz. Citrine, for instance, is yellow quartz, amethyst is violet quartz, and bloodstone is green quartz with red spots. Quartz is an incredibly versatile stone that can be used for many purposes.

Quartz has been used for magical purposes for thousands of years. The 8,000-year-old Egyptian Temple of Hathor contained many beautiful quartz crystals. In 1921, scientists discovered quartz was piezoelectric, which means it can generate an electrical charge.

Clear quartz can be used to help you accomplish your goals and provide you with protection. It can be used for any metaphysical purpose, and should be one of your first purchases.

Rose Quartz (Pink)

Rose quartz is known as the "love stone," as it balances the emotions and promotes love, kindness, and compassion. It is said to increase fertility and promote happy families. It heals anger, frustrations, and disappointment. It enables people to restore faith in their capabilities. If you need to, rose quartz will enable you to forgive yourself.

Smoky Quartz
(Pale, Smoky Gray to Brownish-Gray)

Smoky quartz is one of the most important crystals for grounding and protection. It can absorb large amounts of negative energy and release it into the earth where it can be neutralized.

Smoky quartz can release stress, tension, anxiety, resentments, and emotional problems. It protects the home, vehicle, and possessions from theft and damage.

Selenite (Colorless to Clear White)

Selenite is a soft stone named after Selene, goddess of the moon in Greek mythology. Selenite relates to truth, honesty, and mental clarity. Because of its association to the moon, selenite also relates to love, fertility, intuition, and the subconscious. Selenite is often used for contacting angels and spirit guides.

Tiger's Eye (Golden Brown and Yellow)

Tiger's eye balances the emotions and provides comfort and security. It calms the nerves and improves concentration. Wear tiger's eye whenever you find yourself in a difficult situation and want to know how to handle it.

Black Tourmaline (Striated Black)

Black tourmaline wards off negative energy, no matter where it comes from. It is a protective stone that keeps you grounded and in control. If you carry one in your pocket, others will have no difficulty in understanding you. If you lack a sense of purpose, meditating on a black tourmaline will provide plenty of ideas.

APPENDIX B: ADDITIONAL CRYSTALS BY USE

In time, you may want to add more crystals to your collection. Here are some more crystals, along with their keywords:

Amazonite: soothes nervous system

Aquamarine: mental clarity, spirituality, self-expression

Azurite: expands consciousness, helps healers

Calcite: aids astral travel, balances the body

Diamond: removes negativity and blockages from the body

Emerald: aids psychic work and harmonizes relationships

Garnet: strengthens self-esteem, willpower, and circulation

Iolite: balances body, aids astral travel, provides patience

Jade: cleanses body, provides protection

Moldavite: enlightenment and transformation

Moonstone: receptive, intuitive, and sensitive

Obsidian: reduces tension, protection

Opal: harmony, creativity, and protection

Ruby: leadership, drive, energy, spirituality, and confidence

Sapphire: positivity, intuition

Sodalite: courage, harmony, and communication

Topaz: creativity, understanding, and emotional balance

APPENDIX C:
CRYSTALS BY COLOR

Many people become interested in crystals because of their amazing range of colors.

Red Crystals

Red is the color of courage, energy, passion, strength, will-power, and love.

Bloodstone: courage, persistence, personal power

Red Carnelian: motivation, excitement, abundance

Garnet: strength, willpower, charm, persuasion

Red Jasper: confidence, intelligence, action

Ruby: action, vitality, passion

Orange and Yellow Crystals

Yellow is the color of communication, pleasure, enjoyment, and happiness. Orange is the color of vitality, creativity, and cooperation.

Amber: carefree, vitality, energy

Orange or Yellow Calcite: concentration, intellect, study

Citrine: creativity, imagination, success

Yellow Fluorite: memory, thinking, awareness

Green Crystals

Green is the color of balance, fair-play, and harmony.

Green Aventurine: leadership, success, honesty

Emerald: wisdom, forethought, encouragement

Green Jade: decisiveness, goal-setting, abundance

Malachite: balance, hard work, sleep

Blue Crystals

Blue is the color of adventure, compassion, and intuition.

Blue Lace Agate: peace, charm, serenity

Lapis Lazuli: spirituality, hidden truths, peacefulness

Sapphire: wisdom, learning, abundance

Violet Crystals

Violet and purple are the colors of spirituality, mystery, and high standing.

Amethyst: intuition, peace, spirituality

Purple Fluorite: meditation, intuition, inner peace

White and Clear Crystals

White and clear are the colors that symbolize change and new starts.

Moonstone: healing, intuition, and love

Clear Quartz: balance, purity, concentration

Black Crystals

Black is the color of sophistication and potential.

Jet: strength, protection, persistence

Onyx: strength, forward planning, thought

Black Tourmaline: grounding, steady, thought before action

APPENDIX D: STONES NOT TO USE IN WATER

Amber

Angelite

Azurite

Calcite

Carnelian

Dioptase

Galena

Halite

Hematite

Labradorite

Malachite

Lodestone

Lepidolite

Mica

Moldavite

Moonstone

Obsidian

Opal

Pearl

Pyrite

Selenite

Tiger's Eye

Turquoise

APPENDIX E:
WHAT TO DO IF YOU LOSE
YOUR CRYSTAL

Over the years, I've lost several crystals. Some were simply mislaid and I managed to find them again. However, two vanished without a trace, and I still sometimes wonder where they are now. As many people have told me about their lost crystals, I know that this is a frequent occurrence.

The first thing I do if I lose anything is to sit down, close my eyes, relax by taking several slow, deep breaths, and think about where I was and what I was doing when I last saw whatever it was. I did this recently with a library book that I'd mislaid. I forgot that I'd taken it with me when I visited my sister. I wanted to show her the book, as I thought she'd enjoy reading it. As soon as I closed my eyes and thought about the book, I knew that it was at my sister's home.

This method works well with crystals, too. On one occasion, I'd been meditating with my crystal when the phone rang. I had a lengthy conversation with a friend and then went upstairs to my office. When I needed the crystal a day or two later, I couldn't remember where I'd left it, and a quick search of the usual places where I normally used it revealed nothing. When I closed my eyes, relaxed, and thought about the crystal, the memory of sitting in the armchair in our family room came back to me, and I was able to find it. It had rolled down inside the chair, and wasn't visible, but once I knew where it was, it took only a few seconds to find it.

If nothing comes back to me when I do the relaxation exercise, I use a pendulum to dowse for it (see chapter 34). I start by asking if it's in the house I'm in. Usually it is, and then it's a matter of finding the room it's in, followed by the actual location. Sometimes the crystal will turn up in a room that I haven't visited for a while, and I've no idea how it got there. I have a large collection of tarot cards, and once, my pendulum told me my missing crystal was with them. It was, and to this day I've no idea how that happened. If the pendulum tells me that the missing crystal isn't in my home, I'll ask further questions to try to find the location.

On two occasions, this didn't work, and both times I asked the pendulum if I'd ever see the crystal again. The pendulum said no, and this proved to be the case.

Strangely, I wasn't upset by this. Many years earlier, a wise spiritual lady told me that once a crystal had completed its work, it could vanish and reappear somewhere else to carry on its work with someone who needed it more than I did. This could be a form of teleportation. Whatever the reason, when it happened, her words came back to me, and I found it comforting to know that my crystal had gone to someone who would receive the same benefit from it that I had experienced.

I've lost crystals, but I've also found crystals. Some years ago, I found a small piece of hematite on a busy sidewalk in the center of the city I live in. No one else had noticed it, so I picked it up, knowing that it was meant for me. I assumed that it had belonged to someone who no longer needed it, and it was now offering itself to me.

If you permanently lose a crystal, mentally send it your thanks and blessing. Let it know how much you appreciate what it did for you and how grateful you are for everything it taught you. When you feel ready, choose another crystal.

BIBLIOGRAPHY

Bonewitz, Ra. *Cosmic Crystals*. Wellingborough, UK: Turnstone Press Limited, 1983.

Bowman, Catherine. *Crystal Ascension: Spiritual Growth & Planetary Healing*. St. Paul, MN: Llewellyn Publications, 1996.

———. *Crystal Awareness*. St. Paul, MN: Llewellyn Publications, 1987.

Cunningham, Scott. *Cunningham's Encyclopedia of Crystal, Gem & Metal Magic*. St. Paul, MN: Llewellyn Publications, 1988.

Dale, Cyndi. *Llewellyn's Complete Book of Chakras*. Woodbury, MN: Llewellyn Publications, 2016.

Damisch, Lysann. "Keep Your Fingers Crossed! The Influence of Superstition on Subsequent Task

Performance and Its Mediating Mechanism." 2008. http://citeseerx.ist.psu.edu/viewdoc/download?doi=10. 1.1.850.4924&rep=rep1&type=pdf.

Emoto, Masaru. *The Hidden Messages in Water*. New York: Atria Books, 2001.

Galde, Phyllis. *Crystal Healing: The Next Step*. St. Paul, MN: Llewellyn Publications, 1988.

Gifford, Edward S. *The Charms of Love*. London: Faber & Faber Limited, 1963.

Glazer, A. M. *Crystallography: A Very Short Introduction*. Oxford, UK: Oxford University Press, 2016.

Hall, Judy. *The Crystal Bible*. Hampshire, UK: Godsfield Press, 2003.

———. *Encyclopedia of Crystals*. Vancouver, BC: Fairwinds Press, 2013.

Katzir, Shaul. *The Beginnings of Piezoelectricity: A Study in Mundane Physics*. Dordrecht, Netherlands: Springer, 2006.

Kenner, Corrine. *Crystals for Beginners*. Woodbury, MN: Llewellyn Worldwide, 2006.

Keyte, Geoffrey. *The Mystical Crystal: Expanding Your Crystal Consciousness*. Saffron Walden: The C. W. Daniel Company, 1993.

Knuth, Bruce. *Gems in Myth, Legend and Lore*. Thornton, CA: Jewelers Press, 1999.

Kunz, George Frederick. *The Curious Lore of Precious Stones*. Philadelphia: J. B. Lippincott Company, 1913.

———. *The Magic of Jewels and Charms*. Philadelphia: J. B. Lippincott Company, 1915.

Lembo, Margaret Ann. *The Essential Guide to Crystals, Minerals and Stones*. Woodbury, MN: Llewellyn Worldwide, 2013.

Markham, Ursula. *The Crystal Workbook*. Wellingborough, UK: The Aquarian Press, 1988.

Mégemont, Florence. *The Metaphysical Book of Gems and Crystals*. Rochester, VT: Healing Arts Press, 2008.

Miles, Otesa. "Migraine Statistics." Migraine. com. Published 2010. https://migraine.com/ migraine-statistics/.

Polk, Patti. *The Crystal Guide: Identification, Purpose, Powers and Values*. Iola, WI: Krause Publications, 2016.

Regis, Riza. *Understanding Crystal Power*. Manila, Philippines: InterSelf Foundation. 1999.

Rogo, D. Scott. *Leaving the Body: A Complete Guide to Astral Projection*. Englewood Cliffs, NJ: Prentice-Hall, Inc., 1983.

Rogo, D. Scott, ed. *Mind Beyond the Body: The Mystery of ESP Projection*. New York: Penguin Books, 1978.

Shonin, E., W. Van Gordon, and M. D. Griffiths. "Meditation as Medication: Are Attitudes Changing?" *British Journal of General Practice* 63, no. 654 (December 2013).

Simmons, Robert. *The Pocket Book of Stones: Who They Are & What They Teach*. Berkeley, CA: North Atlantic Books, 2015.

Webster, Richard. *365 Ways to Attract Good Luck*. Woodbury, MN: Llewellyn Publications, 2014.

———. *Astral Travel for Beginners*. St. Paul, MN: Llewellyn Publications, 1998.

———. *Aura Reading for Beginners*. St. Paul, MN: Llewellyn Publications, 1998.

———. *Candle Magic for Beginners*. St. Paul, MN: Llewellyn Publications, 2004.

———. *Pendulum Magic for Beginners*. St. Paul, MN: Llewellyn Worldwide, 2002.

———. *Practical Guide to Past-Life Memories*. St. Paul, MN: Llewellyn Publications, 2001.

———. *Rituals for Beginners*. Woodbury, MN: Llewellyn Publications, 2016.

To Write the Author

If you wish to contact the author or would like more information about this book, please write to the author in care of Llewellyn Worldwide, and we will forward your request. Both the author and the publisher appreciate hearing from you and learning of your enjoyment of this book and how it has helped you. Llewellyn Worldwide cannot guarantee that every letter written to the author can be answered, but all will be forwarded. Please write to:

Richard Webster
⁄ Llewellyn Worldwide
2143 Wooddale Drive
Woodbury, MN 55125-2989

Please enclose a self-addressed stamped envelope for reply, or $1.00 to cover costs. If outside the USA, enclose an international postal reply coupon.

.

Rituals

For Beginners

Simple Ways to Connect to Your Spiritual Side

RICHARD WEBSTER

Rituals for Beginners
Simple Ways to Connect to Your Spiritual Side
RICHARD WEBSTER

Discover simple, meaningful rituals you can use to enrich your life in ways large and small. Join renowned author Richard Webster as he shares ideas for honoring important transitions such as birth and marriage, and for practicing uplifting habits like forgiveness, gratitude, and blessings. Explore tips for making everyday tasks into moments of spiritual connection. Celebrate the changing seasons, develop a closer relationship with the Divine, or create your own rituals based on your innermost feelings and desires. *Rituals for Beginners* also includes techniques for gaining newfound prosperity and attracting the life you want, as you perform ceremonies infused with spiritual meaning.

978-0-7387-4765-1, 312 pp., 5 ¼ x 8   **$14.99**

Crystal
Magic

Mineral Wisdom for Pagans & Wiccans
SANDRA KYNES

Crystal Magic
Mineral Wisdom for Pagans & Wiccans
SANDRA KYNES

Strengthen your connection with the natural world as you learn to incorporate the power of crystals and gemstones into your magical practice. This comprehensive, full-color book is exquisitely designed to be both user-friendly and a gorgeous addition to your bookshelf. Inside, you'll find everything you need to effectively work with crystals, from the history, science, and magic of the mineral kingdom to an encyclopedic list of nearly 200 varieties of stones.

Explore numerous ways to grow your knowledge and skills, including details on buying and preparing stones, magical associations by color, astrological influences, and how to spot fakes. Discover a new, powerful form of crystal grid and which stone is best for a specific goal. With more than 200 color photographs and convenient guides to correspondences, associated deities, and more, *Crystal Magic* will serve as a timeless, indispensable reference.

978-0-7387-5341-6, 312 pp., 7 ½ x 9 ⅛   **24.99**

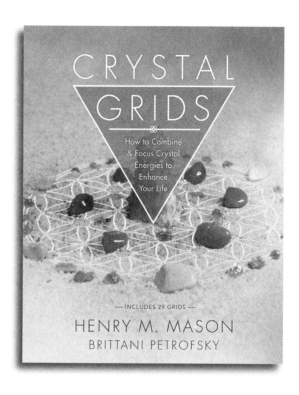

CRYSTAL

GRIDS

How to Combine
& Focus Crystal
Energies to
Enhance
Your Life

— INCLUDES 29 GRIDS —

HENRY M. MASON

BRITTANI PETROFSKY

Crystal Grids
How to Combine & Focus Crystal Energies
to Enhance Your Life
HENRY M. MASON AND BRITTANI PETROFSKY

Crystal grids are effective for transforming your life in a dazzling array of powerful and practical ways. Whether you desire to find love, attract wealth, bless your home, overcome anxiety, or clear negative energy, the crystal grids in this book will help you achieve your goals. With simple instructions and comprehensive insights, *Crystal Grids* shows you how to choose the best crystals for your purpose, select a grid shape that will enhance your intention, clear and position the stones, and activate the grid.

Discover how you can use crystal energy for improved health, wealth, relationships, and a better life. This book also includes twenty-nine expertly designed grids that you can use immediately to reinforce and magnify the power of your crystals.

978-0-7387-4688-3, 216 pp., 7 ½ x 9 ¼   **17.99**

To order, call 1-877-NEW-WRLD or visit llewellyn.com
Prices subject to change without notice